# BRUTUS LEGACY
## FOUNDING BRITAIN'S FUTURE

Richard Simonian

The Patient Chief, who lab'ring long, arriv'd
On Britains Shore and brought with fav'ring Gods
Arts Arms and Honour to her Ancient Sons:
Daughter of Memory! from elder Time
Recall; and me, with Britains Glory fir'd,
Me, far from meaner Care or meaner Song,
Snatch to thy Holy Hill of Spotless Bay,
My Country's Poet, to record her Fame.

# TABLE OF CONTENTS

# INTRODUCTION

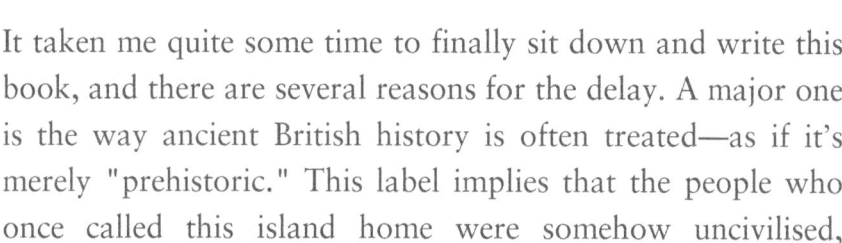

It taken me quite some time to finally sit down and write this book, and there are several reasons for the delay. A major one is the way ancient British history is often treated—as if it's merely "prehistoric." This label implies that the people who once called this island home were somehow uncivilised, without written records, and lacking any connection to the sophisticated societies of mainland Europe.

But nothing could be further from the truth. In the global academic sphere, this limited perspective often prevails, reducing our ancient history to legend, myth, or folklore. For those who use these terms, there's an unspoken suggestion that our past isn't worth taking seriously. This attitude can make one feel almost embarrassed to delve into these eras with any degree of seriousness. Questions naturally arise: Why bother? What could possibly be gained from studying such distant times?

The answer, however, is straightforward: understanding our past is the key to comprehending our present, which in turn helps us shape our future.

I count myself lucky to have grown up in a family, especially on my mother's side, where the telling of historical stories was valued. My grandmother, in particular, brought the past to life for me. Thanks to her, figures like King Arthur and Robin Hood weren't just mythical heroes but tangible parts of our heritage.

As a child, I would often spend holidays with my grandmother, sometimes three or four times a year. During these visits, I spent most of my time in the garden, and between the ages of 10 and 14, I'd fashion my own weapons out of bits of wood I found there. Crafting swords and shields became a cherished pastime, and in the heat of my imagination, I found myself battling against emperors and kings. In those moments, I wasn't just a boy in a garden—I was a victorious leader, reclaiming a forgotten legacy that has always belonged to us.

Curiously, I even had a second-in-command named Colonel, though the reasons behind that name choice have faded with time. Leading armies that included their families became a common

theme in these play sessions. Little did I know back then that these childhood games would, in the years to come, take on a profound significance when delving into our ancient history.

At the age of twelve, I vividly recall a pivotal conversation with my grandmother. She beckoned me inside from the garden, eager to impart knowledge she deemed crucial for me to understand. My grandmother, a woman of few words, commanded our undivided attention whenever she spoke. Her words often held deeper meanings, cloaked in riddles, but always memorable. She had dedicated her life to caring for others, working tirelessly as a nurse, matron, and occupational therapist in a hospital. Yet, on weekends, she embraced her true calling as a 'Peller,' a term used by the West Country folk to describe a woman versed in the ways of the 'cunning folk.'

During this conversation, she revealed the origins of our maternal lineage. She told me our ancestors arrived on this island during the second migration, blending their lives with the aboriginal people. The leader of our group, she proudly recounted, was crowned the first king of the island. They hailed from the Kongo, she said. Years later, I discovered that while much of her story held true, the Kongo connection was more a reflection of the political dynamics of the time. The local aborigines, influenced by the ancient Kongo, derived their laws and directives from that culture.

As I delved deeper into our family history, the layers of our past began to unfold, revealing a tapestry rich with cultural intersections and historical nuances. My grandmother's revelations had ignited a curiosity in me that couldn't be extinguished. I started researching the second migration she mentioned, trying to piece together how our family's journey intersected with the broader historical events of that era.

The more I learned, the more I realised the complexity of our identity. Our ancestors were not just passive recipients of history; they were active participants, shaping their destiny in a new land. This realisation brought a sense of responsibility and pride. I understood that our family story was a microcosm of a larger narrative, one that involved the blending of cultures, the resilience in the face of adversity, and the pursuit of autonomy.

This journey of discovery also led me to explore the ancient Kongo influence she mentioned. It was fascinating to uncover how these distant cultural ties had subtly woven themselves into the fabric of our family's beliefs, customs, and practices. The wisdom of the Kongo, once a political guide for the aborigines, had trickled down through generations, manifesting in the values and traditions that my grandmother and others in our family held dear.

As I pieced together these historical fragments, I couldn't help but feel a deeper connection to my grandmother. Her stories were not just tales of the past; they were the keys to understanding our identity and our place in the world. Her role as a Peller, once a weekend pursuit, now appeared to me as a vital link between our family and the rich heritage we carried.

This exploration of our roots also brought into focus the broader context of our existence on the island. It was a narrative of convergence and divergence, of adopting new lands and adapting old traditions. It was a testament to the enduring human spirit, capable of thriving in the midst of change and maintaining a sense of identity despite the tides of time and history.

In this journey, I came to realise that my grandmother's stories were not just a recollection of the past, but a living, breathing legacy that I was now a part of – a legacy that I was responsible for carrying forward and passing on to the next generation.

As I progress through the pages of this book, readers will encounter various cultural contrasts. In these sections, I discuss spiritual topics that may seem remarkably foreign to contemporary mindsets. However, I believe it's essential to incorporate these perspectives to provide a comprehensive understanding of how our ancestors perceived the world, to the best of my ability to interpret and convey.

I anticipate that many historians might criticise this book, but such scrutiny doesn't concern me. I view this world as one not merely for the layperson, but rather for the initiate - those seeking deeper knowledge and understanding. This perspective stems from a sense that we, as a society, have lost our way.

This book is also a response to those awakening and questioning how we arrived at our current state. The COVID-19 pandemic was a turning point that revealed much about our society. It was disheartening to witness a nation once known for its bravery become submissive, adhering to what I perceived as illogical mandates: compulsory mask-wearing, enforced home confinement, and strict state-regulated movement. Furthermore, the push by the state and various sectors to mandate an experimental vaccine, despite the existence of other options, was particularly troubling. This experience echoes our past struggles with slavery and suggests parallels with the present, as we approach the Agenda 2030 goals. These include the concept of 15-minute cities and a centralised monetary system where rewards hinge on compliance.

Perhaps this book will kindle a passion in its readers, inspiring them to confront their challenges directly and courageously pursue freedom, as we have done in the past. So, let us embark on this journey together...

# HISTORY OF TROY

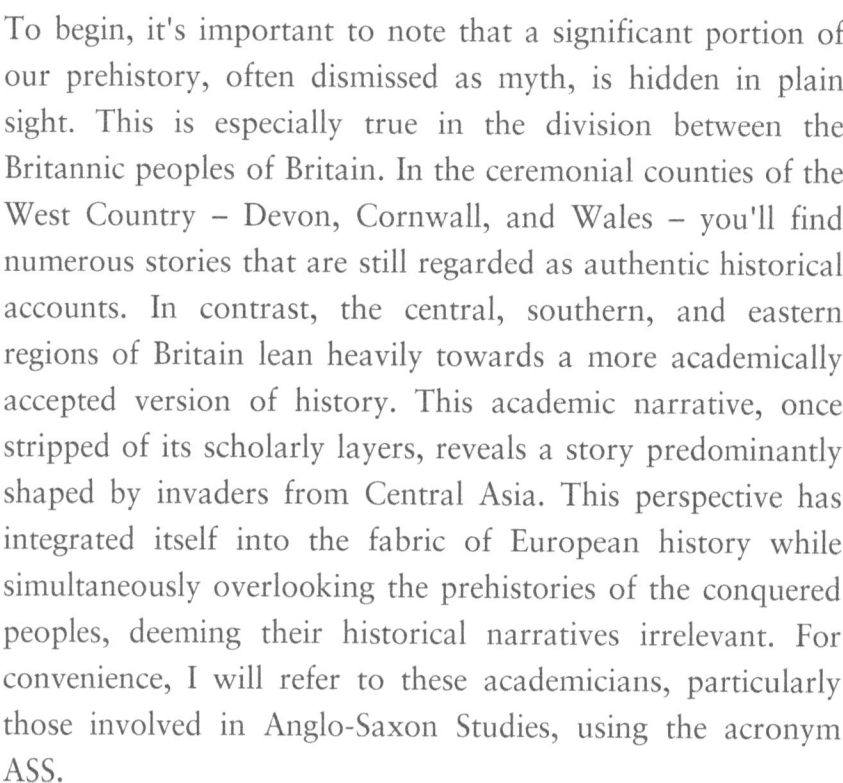

To begin, it's important to note that a significant portion of our prehistory, often dismissed as myth, is hidden in plain sight. This is especially true in the division between the Britannic peoples of Britain. In the ceremonial counties of the West Country – Devon, Cornwall, and Wales – you'll find numerous stories that are still regarded as authentic historical accounts. In contrast, the central, southern, and eastern regions of Britain lean heavily towards a more academically accepted version of history. This academic narrative, once stripped of its scholarly layers, reveals a story predominantly shaped by invaders from Central Asia. This perspective has integrated itself into the fabric of European history while simultaneously overlooking the prehistories of the conquered peoples, deeming their historical narratives irrelevant. For convenience, I will refer to these academicians, particularly those involved in Anglo-Saxon Studies, using the acronym ASS.

Regarding the discovery of ancient Troy, credit goes to Heinrich Schliemann, a German businessman and archaeology pioneer. His late 19th-century work, driven by a fascination with Homer's "The Iliad" and "The Odyssey," sought to validate their historical veracity. In the 1870s, Schliemann commenced excavations in Hissarlik, northwestern Turkey, convinced it was the site of ancient Troy. His work unveiled a succession of ancient cities built upon one another, dating back millennia. Despite criticisms of his methods, Schliemann's findings at Hissarlik were groundbreaking and foundational for modern archaeology.

While Schliemann's identification of Hissarlik as Troy is widely accepted, some debate remains. Further archaeological evidence, notably from Carl Blegen in the 1930s, has supported Schliemann's claim. Yet, whether Hissarlik is indeed the exact location of Troy continues to be a subject of scholarly discussion.

Schliemann's theory was influenced by earlier suggestions from Scottish journalist Charles Maclaren in 1822 and archaeologist Frank Calvert, who had started excavations at Hissarlik before Schliemann's arrival. Schliemann, inspired by Homer's descriptions of the surrounding region and proximity to the Aegean Sea, theorised that Troy was located in northwest Asia Minor (today's Turkey).

From a different historical perspective, Welsh bard Iolo Morganwg (Edward Williams) offered intriguing insights in his published Triads of Britain in Y Myvyrian Archaiology in 1807. Although often criticised and labeled a forger and fantasist by members of the British ASS, Morganwg accessed numerous manuscripts, including those from private gentry estates. Displaying a moment of bardic brilliance, he penned a sentence that subtly guided readers toward understanding their origins: "The first was Hu the Mighty, who brought the nation of the Cambrians first to the Isle of Britain; and they came from the Summer Country, which is also called Defrobani (that is, where Constantinople now stands); and they came over the Hazy Sea to the Isle of Britain, and to Armorica, where they settled." This statement adds a layer of clarity to our understanding of the ancient Britons' origins.

Putting this under analysis most notably speaking of the first nation coming from Defrobani where a similar sounding name Taprobane is an ancient name for a place often identified with the island of Sri Lanka. The marine kingdom of the mermaid and mermen, a historical creature often described as being half fish and half woman or half man, and it is associated with Taprobane. Mermaids are historical beings found in many cultures' around the world, and their descriptions can vary significantly. These creatures are often portrayed as beautiful and enchanting, sometimes luring sailors with their singing and beauty, and are a common subject in maritime history.

The specific association of mermaids with Taprobane (Sri Lanka) reflects the long-standing tradition of maritime stories and histories of the people in the Indian or Andaman Ocean region. The Tamil people of Sri Lanka are one of the most oldest aboriginal people on the earth part of the 'Dra'-'Vida' of southern India where the 'land is bounded by the three oceans'.

Before the name Constantinople emerged in Asia Minor—once part of Greater Armenia—the city was simply known in Armenian as "The City" Պոլիս (Bolis) later it was called by the name as Բիւզանդիոն (Byuzandion), closely aligning with the Greek term. Byzantium (Greek: Βυζάντιον, Byzántion): This was the original name given by the Greek colonists. It remained known as Byzantium until the Roman Emperor Constantine the Great re-founded it as Constantinople in 330 A.D.

The Greek name Byzantion and the city of Troy (Greek: Τροία, Troía; also known as Ilion, Ἴλιον) Ilion or Iliad from Homer are the same but they do not share direct linguistic similarities. However, there are some thematic links between Byzantium (later Constantinople) and Troy in cultural and historical narratives:

- **Geographical Proximity:** Byzantium was situated near the ancient city of Troy, located across the Dardanelles Strait. This close proximity allowed for a significant cultural and historical connection between the two cities.

- **Historical Connections:** Both cities held legendary and symbolic status within Greek and Roman History. For instance, after the fall of Troy, Aeneas, a Trojan hero, was said to have founded a new lineage that would eventually lead to the establishment of Rome. In later Roman History, Byzantium was seen as a kind of eastern counterpart to Rome, linking it indirectly to the heritage of                                  Troy.

- **Historical Successor:** With the establishment of Constantinople as the capital of the Byzantine Empire, it was sometimes referred to in the context of being a "New Troy" or "New Rome." The city represented a continuation of the ancient cultural and political heritage from Troy through Rome to Byzantium. Let us Begin at the beginning by telling the story of the generations of Brutus and the creation of Troy. Our Indigenous history.

## Disclaimer

This book was written with the heartfelt intention of preserving and sharing the great and glorious past of our people. While it does not claim to be an academic text, nor has it been formally proofread by scholarly institutions, it is a work of dedication, drawn from history, tradition, and the enduring legacy of our ancestors. My purpose in writing this is not to present a rigid academic analysis, but to offer a story that can be passed down through generations—a book for families to read together, to spark curiosity, and to remind us all of the strength, resilience, and noble heritage that shaped our land.

May this book serve as a beacon, reigniting pride in our history and inspiring future generations to carry forth the spirit of our ancestors with honour and wisdom.

# THE BIRTH OF THE WORLD

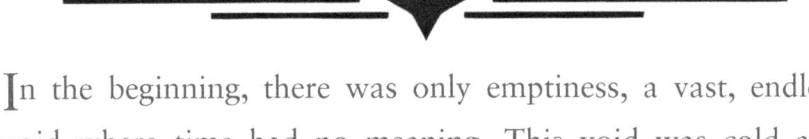

In the beginning, there was only emptiness, a vast, endless void where time had no meaning. This void was cold and silent, a place of stillness and potential. From this nothingness, something stirred. It was Chaos, the first spark of life, though life was too strong a word. Chaos was more a feeling than a being, a whisper of what was to come.

From Chaos, in a mysterious and unknowable way, there emerged Gaia. She was the Earth, solid and strong, nurturing yet fierce. Gaia was alone, but she was not lonely. She revealed in her own power, in the soil and stone that made up her being. But as time passed, she longed for something more, and from her longing, Uranus was born. Uranus was the Sky, vast and infinite, stretching over Gaia like a protective lover.

Gaia and Uranus were inseparable. They brought forth life together, their union producing the Titans, beings of immense strength and will. Among them was Cronus, the youngest and most ambitious. Cronus was different from his siblings. He was restless, always looking to the horizon, never satisfied with his lot. His eyes were filled with a yearning for power, for freedom from the shadow of his father.

# THE RISE OF CRONUS

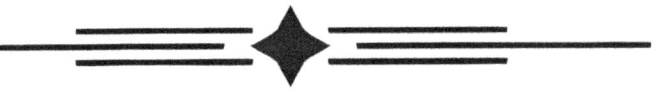

Uranus, fearing the power of his children, sought to keep them under control. He saw their potential as a threat, and he kept them close, refusing to let them explore the world Gaia had given them. This angered Gaia, who loved her children and wanted them to thrive. She whispered to Cronus in the dark of the night, planting the seed of rebellion in his heart.

Cronus, with Gaia's help, overthrew Uranus in a violent struggle, using a sickle forged from the very earth that was his mother. As Uranus fell, he cursed Cronus, foretelling that Cronus, too, would be overthrown by his own child.

Cronus took the throne, but he could not escape his father's curse. Every time his wife, Rhea, bore a child, Cronus would feel a knot of fear tighten in his stomach. He would take the newborn, gaze into its innocent eyes, and swallow it whole, hoping to thwart the prophecy. One by one, his children vanished into the darkness of his own making.

But Rhea could not bear to lose another child. When her youngest, Zeus, was born, she hid him away, giving Cronus a stone wrapped in swaddling clothes instead. Zeus grew up in secret, nurtured by the whispers of the wind and the strength of the earth, until the day came when he was ready to challenge his father.

# THE BATTLE FOR THE WORLD

Zeus returned, his heart burning with the desire for justice and the need to free his siblings. He confronted Cronus, who was now old and weary, haunted by his own actions. The battle that followed shook the earth and the sky. It was a clash not just of strength, but of wills—of a young god's hope for a new world against an old god's fear of change.

With the help of his siblings, whom he freed from Cronus's belly, Zeus triumphed. The Titans were defeated and cast into the depths of Tartarus, and Zeus took his place as the ruler of the cosmos. But Zeus was not like his father. He ruled with wisdom, though he was not without flaws. His reign brought order to the world, yet it was a world still full of challenges and struggles.

# DARDANUS'S JOURNEY

Zeus, in his moments of solitude, reflected on the power he now held. He understood that true strength lay not just in force, but in the ability to nurture and protect. This understanding led to his union with Electra, one of the Pleiades, and together they had a son, Dardanus.

Dardanus was born with the wanderlust of his father and the grace of his mother. He was a child of destiny, though he did not know it. As he grew, he felt a pull toward lands far from his home. The stories of old gods and ancient battles whispered in his ears, urging him to seek out a place where he could build something of his own.

He traveled across seas and mountains, eventually arriving in the rugged lands of Asia Minor. There, he met Teucer, a wise and aged king who saw in Dardanus the potential for greatness. Teucer offered him his daughter, Batia, in marriage, and with her hand, the promise of a future.

Dardanus accepted, and with Batia by his side, he founded the kingdom of Dardania. It was a harsh land, but Dardanus loved it fiercely. He taught his people how to build, to farm, and to worship the gods. His kingdom grew, and with it, his legend. He was not just a king; he was a father to his people, guiding them with a steady hand and a heart full of hope.

# THE LEGACY OF TROS

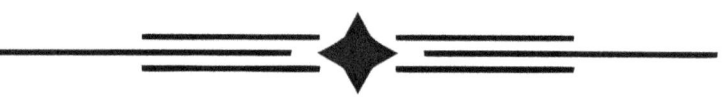

Dardanus's son, Erichthonius, inherited his father's kingdom and his love for the land. Erichthonius was known for his wealth, not just in gold and silver, but in wisdom and strength. He expanded the kingdom, securing alliances and building a legacy that would outlast him.

Erichthonius's son, Tros, was destined to take this legacy even further. Tros was a man of vision, seeing in the land of Dardania the seeds of something greater. He founded the city of Troy, naming it after himself, and began to build its walls. He knew that Troy could be a beacon of civilisation, a place where the gods themselves would come to visit.

Tros had three sons: Ilus, Assaracus, and Ganymede. Each was blessed by the gods, but it was Ilus who would carry the weight of his father's dream. Ilus was a man of courage and ambition, eager to prove himself worthy of his heritage.

Ilus and the Foundation of Ilium

Ilus, driven by a desire to carve out his own place in the world, left Troy and journeyed to Phrygia. There, he won the favour of the king in a contest of skill, earning a spotted cow as his prize. The king told Ilus to follow the cow and build a city where it lay down. Ilus did as he was told, and the cow led him to the plains near the Scamander River.

There, in the quiet of the evening, with the sun setting behind the distant hills, the cow lay down. Ilus knelt beside it, placing his hands on the earth. He could feel the heartbeat of the land, the promise of what could be. This was where he would build his city—a city that would stand for generations, a testament to the strength of his lineage.

Ilus prayed to the gods for protection, and they answered by sending down the Palladium, a sacred statue of Athena. As long as the Palladium remained in the city, it would be invincible. With this divine blessing, Ilus began the work of building Ilium, the city that would later be known as Troy.

# THE GROWING POWER OF TROY

Under Ilus's guidance, Troy grew from a small settlement into a mighty city. The walls rose high, strong and impenetrable, a symbol of the city's power and the favour of the gods. The people of Troy flourished, their culture and influence spreading far beyond the city's walls.

But with power came envy, and Troy's enemies began to multiply. Ilus was aware of the dangers that lurked beyond his city, but he was determined to protect what he had built. He ruled with wisdom, always looking for ways to strengthen his city and his people.

As the years passed, Ilus grew older, and he knew that his time was coming to an end. But he took comfort in knowing that his legacy would live on through his children and their children after them. The city of Troy would stand as a monument to his life, a place where the gods walked among men, where dreams could be forged into reality.

# INTRODUCTION TO LAOMEDON

The city of Troy was still young, its walls newly risen, yet they already cast long shadows over the plains by the Scamander River. The hum of life within the city was vibrant—merchants haggled in the markets, children played in the dusty streets, and the clang of blacksmiths' hammers echoed through the air. This was the city that Ilus had built, a dream of stone and mortar that had become a reality. But for Laomedon, the son of Ilus, this was just the beginning.

Laomedon had always known that one day he would sit on Troy's throne, but as a boy, that knowledge was more of a burden than a blessing. His father, Ilus, was a giant in his eyes—both figuratively and literally. Ilus's hands, calloused and scarred from years of labor, had shaped the very walls that surrounded them. He was a man of few words but immense presence, and Laomedon often felt like a mere shadow in his father's wake.

Growing up, Laomedon was driven by a fierce determination, though not always in the ways one might expect of a future king. He was known to be stubborn, often challenging his father's decisions, seeking to prove himself in whatever way he could. He would climb the walls of Troy, testing their strength with his own hands, as if trying to understand the weight of responsibility that would one day be his.

Yet, despite his youthful defiance, Laomedon admired his father deeply. He watched Ilus with keen eyes, learning not just how to rule, but how to build—a skill he knew would be essential if Troy was to stand the test of time. Laomedon understood that Troy's future rested not just on its foundations but on its walls, and he became obsessed with the idea of making them impregnable.

When Ilus finally passed, leaving the throne to his son, Laomedon felt a mix of grief and trepidation. He was no longer just the heir; he was now the king. The weight of Troy's future rested on his shoulders, and he felt it every day. The people looked to him not just for leadership, but for protection, and Laomedon was determined not to fail them.

But as he walked through the streets of his city, Laomedon couldn't shake the feeling that Troy, as it was, wasn't enough. His father had laid the groundwork, but Laomedon's vision stretched far beyond what Ilus had ever dreamed. He saw Troy not just as a city of men but as a city that could rival even the homes of the gods. The walls needed to be higher, stronger, more magnificent—so that no one, not even the gods themselves, could bring them down.

In those early days of his reign, Laomedon's ambition burned bright. He was determined to make Troy the greatest city the world had ever seen, a fortress that would stand eternal. But ambition is a double-edged sword, and as

Laomedon would soon learn, the path to greatness is fraught with peril.

# LAOMEDON'S
## ASCENSION TO THE THRONE

The death of Ilus cast a heavy pall over Troy. The city, usually alive with the sounds of daily life, now echoed with a somber quiet. Laomedon stood at the edge of his father's funeral pyre, the heat of the flames biting at his face, though it did little to warm the cold knot of grief in his chest. He had known this day would come, but nothing had prepared him for the reality of it. Ilus, the man who had shaped Troy from the earth itself, was gone, and with him, a part of Laomedon's own identity seemed to have vanished.

The transition of power was seamless in name, but in practice, it was anything but. Laomedon was now king, the weight of the crown settling heavily on his brow. The people of Troy looked to him with a mix of expectation and uncertainty. They had respected Ilus, revered him even, and now they wondered—could his son fill his shoes?

Laomedon felt the pressure keenly. He had always been a man of strong will, but this was different. This was not just about proving himself to his father or the people; this was about securing the future of Troy. He was no longer the brash youth challenging his father's decisions; he was the king, and every choice he made from now on would shape the destiny of his city.

In the days following Ilus's death, Laomedon spent hours alone in the palace, pacing the marble floors as he wrestled with his thoughts. His father's advisors whispered in the halls, offering counsel and caution, but their words only served to remind him of the void left by Ilus. Laomedon knew he had to step out of his father's shadow, to make a name for himself, but how?

Troy was still a young city, it's foundations strong but its future uncertain.

Laomedon knew that the city's strength lay in its walls—those towering barriers that had kept enemies at bay. But he also knew that Troy was vulnerable. The world beyond its walls was vast and filled with dangers—other kingdoms, rival cities, and even the unpredictable whims of the gods.

Laomedon's vision for Troy was clear in his mind: the city must be fortified, expanded, made invincible. It was not enough for Troy to be strong; it had to be unassailable. He could see it—walls so high and thick that no army could breach them, defences so formidable that no enemy would dare to attack.

But turning this vision into reality was another matter. The city's coffers were not limitless, and the people were already burdened by the taxes needed to maintain what they had. There were those in his council who urged caution, advising that Troy should focus on consolidating its current strength rather than reaching for more. But Laomedon was not one to be swayed by caution.

He began to speak of his plans openly, sharing his vision with his advisors, the builders, and the people. He described a Troy that would be the envy of the world, a city so grand and powerful that it would rival even the splendour of the gods. But as he spoke, he could see the doubt in their eyes. They respected him as their king, but they had yet to see if he could lead them as his father had.

The first challenge came quickly. The neighbouring kingdoms, sensing the change in leadership, began testing Troy's borders, probing for weakness. Laomedon responded with a mix of diplomacy and force, asserting Troy's strength while maintaining a veneer of peace. But he knew this was only the beginning. To truly secure Troy, he needed to act on his vision.

Laomedon called upon the finest architects and builders in the land, tasking them with the monumental job of expanding the city's walls. He poured resources into the project, diverting funds from other areas, much to the chagrin of some of his advisors. But Laomedon was relentless. He spent days at the construction site, overseeing every detail, speaking with the workers, and ensuring that his vision was being realised.

As the walls began to rise, so too did Laomedon's confidence. The people, seeing the king's dedication, began to rally behind him. The doubts that had lingered in their minds started to fade as they watched the city grow stronger before their eyes. Laomedon, for all his ambition, was proving himself to be a leader in his own right.

Yet, with every stone laid, Laomedon felt the weight of his responsibilities grow heavier. He knew that he was gambling Troy's future on his vision, and the stakes were high. Failure was not an option, but success was far from guaranteed. As the walls reached ever higher, Laomedon found himself often alone at night, staring out over the city from the palace balcony, wondering if he was making the right choices, if he was truly the king that Troy needed.

But there was no turning back. Laomedon had committed himself to this path, and he would see it through to the end. Troy would be more than just a city—it would be a fortress, a beacon, a testament to his reign. And in those quiet moments, when doubt threatened to creep in, Laomedon would remind himself of the words his father once told him: "A king is not remembered for the peace he keeps, but for the strength he builds."

With that thought, Laomedon would straighten his shoulders, clench his fists, and return to his work, determined to fulfil his destiny and secure Troy's place in history.

# THE BUILDING OF TROY'S WALLS: DIVINE ASSISTANCE

As the days turned into months and the months into years, Laomedon's ambition for Troy grew ever larger. The walls were rising, but not quickly enough to satisfy the king. He knew that time was not on his side—Troy's enemies were many, and the gods themselves were unpredictable. He needed more than just mortal hands to build the walls that would secure his city's future.

Late one evening, as Laomedon walked along the half-built ramparts, his mind raced with worry. The workers were skilled, but the task was monumental, and progress was slow. The walls were strong, but in Laomedon's eyes, they were not yet the impenetrable fortress he envisioned. He felt the weight of his father's legacy on his shoulders and the expectations of his people pressing down on him like never before.

It was during one of these solitary walks that Laomedon encountered two strangers. They were dressed simply, their faces weathered by the sun, and they carried the tools of labourers—hammers, chisels, and the like. They seemed out of place, wandering the construction site at such a late hour. Laomedon, ever suspicious of strangers in his city, approached them.

"What business do you have here at this hour?" Laomedon demanded, his voice carrying the authority of a king.

The taller of the two men, with eyes that seemed to shimmer with a light of their own, looked at Laomedon and smiled. "We've heard of your great work, King Laomedon, and we've come to offer our help."

Laomedon was taken aback by the man's confidence. "And who are you to offer help with a task as grand as this?"

The second man, shorter and broader, spoke in a deep, calming voice. "We are but humble workers, skilled in the art of building. We can help you raise these walls to heights you have only dreamed of."

Laomedon, ever pragmatic, was skeptical. The work was delicate, requiring expertise beyond that of ordinary labourers. Yet there was something about these men—something in their eyes, in their presence—that made him pause. "If you can indeed help, then prove it. Show me what you can do."

The two men exchanged a glance, as if sharing a private joke, then nodded. Without another word, they set to work. Laomedon watched as they moved with an ease and grace that was almost otherworldly. They lifted stones that should have taken several men to carry, fitting them into place as if they were mere pebbles. The sound of their hammers striking the stone was like music, each blow resonating with a power that seemed to vibrate through the very earth beneath them.

Hours passed, but the men did not tire. By dawn, they had completed more in one night than Laomedon's entire workforce could have achieved in a week. The walls stood higher and stronger, the stones fitting together so seamlessly that it seemed they had been carved from a single massive rock. Laomedon was astonished. These were no ordinary men.

The next day, Laomedon sought out the strangers. He found them still working, their pace as relentless as it had been the night before. "Who are you?" he asked, his voice filled with a mixture of awe and suspicion. "No mortal man works as you do."

The taller man, pausing in his labor, turned to Laomedon and smiled. "You are right to question us, King Laomedon. We are not merely men, but gods in disguise. I am Poseidon, god of the sea, and this is Apollo, god of the sun and of prophecy. We have come to aid you in your time of need, to build walls that will stand for all time."

Laomedon's heart raced. He had heard tales of the gods walking among men, but never had he imagined that they would come to his aid. The gravity of the moment weighed on him, but so too did the opportunity. With the gods themselves helping him, Troy's walls would be unmatched in all the world. "Why would you, gods of Olympus, aid me in this task?" Laomedon asked, his voice trembling with a mix of reverence and curiosity.

Poseidon's expression grew serious. "The gods have their reasons, reasons that are not always clear to men. But know this, Laomedon: we see your ambition, your desire to protect your city, and we respect it. In return for our aid, you must promise to offer us a sacrifice, to honour the work we have done here."

Laomedon, though eager to accept their help, felt a flicker of unease. The gods were not known for their kindness; their demands could be harsh, their wrath unforgiving. But the vision of Troy's future—the impregnable city, the shining beacon of power—was too strong to ignore. "I will honour your work," Laomedon promised. "Whatever you ask, I will provide."

With that, the gods continued their work, and Laomedon watched as Troy's walls grew taller, thicker, and more formidable than he had ever dreamed. The people of Troy marvelled at the sight, they're awe mixed with a sense of reverence for the unseen forces that now clearly guided their king.

Days turned into weeks, and soon the work was complete. The walls of Troy stood as a testament to the combined efforts of mortals and gods, a fortress that seemed to reach towards the heavens themselves. Laomedon could hardly believe it—his vision had been realised, and Troy was now the greatest city in the world.

But with the completion of the walls came the time to fulfil his promise. Poseidon and Apollo, having completed their work, came to Laomedon and reminded him of his vow. "We have done as you asked," Apollo said, his voice gentle but firm. "Now it is your turn to keep your word."

Laomedon, however, had begun to feel the intoxicating power of his new position. The walls were complete, the city was safe, and he was its king. The fear that had once driven him to seek the gods' help had dissipated, replaced by a growing arrogance. He looked at the gods, their divine forms now revealed, and a thought crept into his mind: they were no longer needed.

"I thank you for your work," Laomedon said carefully, "but I see no reason to pay a price for something that is now done. The walls are built, and Troy is secure. That should be enough."

Poseidon's eyes darkened, and the air seemed to grow heavy with tension. "You dare to break your promise, mortal?" he thundered. "We have given you a gift beyond measure, and you repay us with deceit?"

Laomedon, emboldened by his success, stood his ground. "Troy is now impenetrable," he replied. "I fear neither man nor god. The walls will stand, with or without your blessing."

Apollo, his gaze sorrowful, turned away. "You have made a grave mistake, Laomedon," he said quietly. "The gods do not forget such slights."

With that, the gods departed, leaving Laomedon alone with his new walls—and the seeds of his own destruction.

# LAOMEDON'S BETRAYAL: REFUSING PAYMENT TO THE GODS

As the last stones were set into the walls of Troy, Laomedon stood at the top of the highest tower, surveying the city below. The view was breathtaking. The walls, now complete, encircled the city like a protective embrace, their sheer size and strength unmatched by any other fortress in the known world. The people of Troy went about their daily lives with a renewed sense of security, their faith in Laomedon stronger than ever. Yet, as Laomedon looked out over his kingdom, a darker emotion began to take root in his heart—pride.

The gods had promised him walls that would make Troy invincible, and they had delivered. But as the days passed, Laomedon began to question whether he truly owed them anything in return. After all, was it not his own vision that had driven the project? His leadership that had marshalled the resources, rallied the workers, and ensured the walls were built? The more he thought about it, the more Laomedon convinced himself that the gods had simply played a minor role in his grand plan.

Laomedon's advisors, sensing his growing arrogance, cautioned him to fulfill his promise to Poseidon and Apollo. "The gods do not take lightly to broken oaths," one advisor warned. "We are only mortals, and our power is fleeting compared to theirs."

But Laomedon dismissed their concerns with a wave of his hand. "Troy is no longer just a city; it is a fortress, a monument to our strength. The gods may have helped, but it is we who will live within these walls, we who will defend them. Why should we bow to them now that the work is done?"

In truth, Laomedon's decision was driven by more than just pride. The construction of the walls had drained Troy's coffers, and the treasury was running low. The sacrifices the gods demanded were no small matter—they required wealth, livestock, and precious offerings that would further strain the city's resources. Laomedon reasoned that the people of Troy would benefit more from keeping these resources within the city than from offering them to distant, unseen deities.

But deeper still, there was a more troubling motivation—Laomedon had begun to believe that Troy was untouchable. The walls, so grand and imposing, seemed to stand as proof that no force, divine or mortal, could bring them down. Laomedon saw himself as the master of his own fate, the king who had defied the odds and built a city that would endure for all time. In his mind, the gods were no longer necessary, their threats hollow in the face of Troy's newfound power.

When Poseidon and Apollo returned to Troy, expecting to receive the payment they had been promised, they found a king who was no longer humble or grateful. Laomedon greeted them with a smile that did not reach his eyes, his words smooth but empty. "I thank you for your help in building these walls," he said, "but Troy has given much already. The city is in need of its resources, and I cannot afford to part with them now."

Poseidon's eyes flashed with anger, the calm blue of the sea replaced by a stormy rage. "You made an oath, Laomedon," he growled, his voice like the rumble of distant thunder. "Do not think that you can break it without consequence."

Apollo, ever the more temperate of the two, placed a hand on Poseidon's arm, though his own eyes were filled with disappointment. "Do you think yourself above the gods, Laomedon?" he asked quietly. "Do you believe that these walls, mighty as they are, can protect you from the wrath you invite by betraying us?"

But Laomedon's arrogance had taken full hold of him. He straightened his back, looking down at the two gods as if they were mere men. "Troy stands stronger now than ever before," he declared. "These walls are impenetrable. The gods may have helped build them, but it is my will that has made Troy what it is. I will not bow to you, nor will I pay a price for something that is already mine."

Poseidon's rage could no longer be contained. The ground beneath Laomedon's feet trembled, and a distant roar of waves crashing against unseen shores filled the air. "You fool," Poseidon hissed. "You think yourself safe behind these walls, but you have built your city on the shifting sands of your own pride. The sea is patient, but it does not forgive."

Apollo, his face now a mask of sorrow, turned his back on Laomedon. "You have chosen your path," he said softly. "But know this: the gods remember, and so does fate."

With those words, the gods vanished, leaving Laomedon standing alone atop his mighty walls. For a moment, a flicker of doubt crossed his mind, a brief shadow that passed over his heart. But it was quickly replaced by the intoxicating sense of power that had fueled his betrayal. Troy was safe. The walls were strong. What could the gods do to him now?

Yet even as he descended from the tower, returning to the life of luxury and power that awaited him within the city, the first seeds of his downfall had already been sown. The betrayal of the gods was not a debt that could be easily forgotten, and the walls of Troy, though mighty, could not protect Laomedon from the consequences of his own hubris.

# THE IMPLICATIONS OF BETRAYAL

Laomedon's refusal to pay the gods was more than just a broken promise—it was a reflection of the man he had become. His pride, which had once driven him to protect and expand his city, had now grown into something darker. He no longer saw himself as a servant of the gods, or even as a king among men. In his eyes, he was something greater, a ruler who had transcended the need for divine favor.

This arrogance blinded him to the reality of his situation. The walls of Troy, though strong, were not invincible. They were built with the help of the very gods he had now betrayed, and without their protection, those walls would stand on foundations as fragile as his own ego. Laomedon had chosen to believe in his own invulnerability, but in doing so, he had exposed himself to dangers far greater than any he had faced before.

The people of Troy, unaware of the storm brewing on the horizon, continued to live their lives within the safety of the walls. They trusted in their king, believed in the strength of the city he had built. But Laomedon's betrayal had set into motion forces that neither he nor his people could control. The gods, once their allies, were now their enemies, and the wrath of the divine was not something that could be easily withstood.

In the days that followed, Laomedon would continue to rule with the same confidence and pride, unaware that the very walls he had fought so hard to build were now the symbols of his greatest mistake. For in turning his back on the gods, Laomedon had sealed his fate, and the fate of Troy, with a single, irrevocable act of betrayal.

# THE WRATH OF THE GODS: DIVINE RETRIBUTION

In the days following Laomedon's refusal to honour his promise to Poseidon and Apollo, the city of Troy remained serene on the surface. The walls stood tall and imposing, and the people continued their lives under the assumption that their king had secured their future. But beneath this façade of calm, an uneasy tension began to simmer—a tension that would soon erupt into chaos.

Poseidon, the god of the sea, did not forget the slight. From the depths of his watery domain, he watched the city with cold, calculating eyes. The sea, which had always been a source of life and sustenance for Troy, began to churn with a new, menacing energy. The fishermen were the first to notice the change. Their nets, once full of fish, came up empty, and the waves that lapped at the shores grew restless, their once soothing rhythm replaced by a relentless pounding that echoed through the night.

Then, one morning, as the sun rose over the horizon, a shadow appeared on the water—a shape unlike anything the people of Troy had ever seen. It was a creature born of nightmares, a massive sea monster sent by Poseidon himself. Its scales glistened like blackened steel, and its eyes burned with the fury of the god who had unleashed it. The monster moved with terrifying grace, its massive body cutting through the waves as it made its way toward the city.

Panic spread like wildfire as the monster approached. The people, who had once placed their faith in the strength of Troy's walls, now found themselves facing a threat they could not comprehend, let alone defend against. The creature reached the shores of Troy, its roar shaking the very foundations of the city. With a single swipe of its massive tail, it smashed through the docks, sending ships and debris flying into the air. The water surged inward, flooding the lower parts of the city, dragging homes and lives into the sea.

Laomedon, standing atop the walls, watched in horror as the monster laid waste to his city. The sight of it—the embodiment of Poseidon's wrath—was a brutal reminder of the power he had so arrogantly dismissed. But even as the destruction unfolded before him, Laomedon's pride refused to let him admit his mistake. He ordered his soldiers to attack the creature, to drive it back into the sea, but their efforts were in vain. The monster was impervious to their weapons, and each attempt to stop it only seemed to enrage it further.

While the monster ravaged the city from the sea, another calamity struck from within. Apollo, the god of the sun and of healing, had once been a protector of Troy, his warmth and light a blessing upon the city. But now, his anger matched that of Poseidon, and he unleashed his fury in the form of a plague—a sickness that spread through the city like a shadow.

It began slowly, almost unnoticed at first. A few coughs here, a fever there. But within days, the sickness had taken hold, striking down rich and poor alike. The air grew thick with the scent of illness, the once-bustling markets now silent as people barricaded themselves in their homes,

hoping to escape the invisible killer. But there was no escape. The plague showed no mercy, claiming the lives of the young and old, the strong and weak, without discrimination.

Laomedon, desperate to save his city, summoned the healers and priests, demanding they find a way to end the suffering. But their remedies were powerless against the divine curse. The more Laomedon tried to assert control, the more the situation spiralled beyond his reach. The people began to whisper in the streets, their faith in their king crumbling as quickly as the city around them. How could this happen? they asked. How could their great king, who had built such mighty walls, have failed them so completely?

The suffering of the people was immense. Families were torn apart by the plague, mothers weeping over the bodies of their children, fathers digging graves for their loved ones. The streets, once filled with life and laughter, became a place of mourning and fear. And all the while, the sea monster continued its assault, each new wave bringing fresh destruction.

Laomedon, once so confident in his ability to protect Troy, now found himself trapped in a nightmare of his own making. He retreated to the palace, where he paced the halls, his mind racing for a solution. But there was none. The gods had turned against him, and there was no undoing what he had set into motion. The walls that had once symbolised Troy's strength now felt like a prison, closing in around him as the weight of his betrayal became unbearable.

In his desperation, Laomedon attempted to appease the gods, offering sacrifices and prayers, but it was too late. Poseidon and Apollo had already passed judgment, and their wrath was not easily quelled. Each new offering was met with silence, the gods refusing to hear the pleas of a king who had so blatantly disregarded their power.

The people, who had once looked to Laomedon for guidance, now saw him as the source of their suffering. Their whispers turned to anger, and that anger soon grew into open rebellion. Laomedon's grip on his throne weakened as the city descended into chaos, the bonds that held Troy together unraveling under the strain of divine retribution.

In the end, Laomedon was left with nothing but the realisation of his own hubris. The city he had sought to protect, the walls he had built with such pride, were now the very symbols of his downfall. The gods had shown him that no mortal, no matter how powerful, could escape their wrath. And as Troy burned, Laomedon was forced to confront the bitter truth: his pride had destroyed the very thing he had sought to preserve.

# THE SACRIFICE OF HESIONE: THE SEA MONSTER AND THE HERO

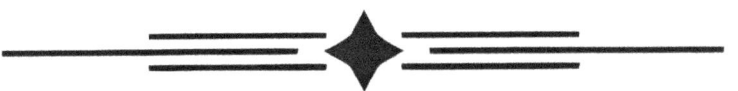

Troy was a city on the brink of despair. The once-proud walls, which had stood as a symbol of strength and security, now loomed like a constant reminder of the gods' wrath. The sea monster continued its relentless assault, battering the city's shores and dragging more lives into the depths. The plague, unleashed by Apollo, had turned Troy into a place of mourning, with each day bringing fresh losses. The people's faith in their king had crumbled, and Laomedon himself was a man haunted by the consequences of his own hubris.

Amidst this chaos, a whisper began to spread through the city—one born of desperation and fear. The people, huddled in their homes, spoke in hushed tones about an ancient practice, a way to appease the anger of the gods: a human sacrifice. Laomedon had heard these whispers, but he had dismissed them at first, refusing to believe that it would come to this. But as the destruction continued and his options dwindled, the idea took root in his mind, growing stronger with each passing day.

One evening, as the sun dipped low on the horizon, casting a red glow over the stormy seas, Laomedon stood on the palace balcony, looking out over the city. The destruction was unimaginable, and he felt the weight of it pressing down on him like a physical force. He had tried everything—offerings, prayers, pleas—but nothing had worked. The gods had turned their backs on him, and now it seemed that only the most extreme measures could save Troy.

His thoughts turned to his daughter, Hesione. She was his most cherished child, the light in his life during these dark days. Hesione had always been gentle and kind, beloved by the people for her compassion. Laomedon's heart ached at the thought of losing her, but he was a king before he was a father. And as a king, he had a duty to his people, even if that duty meant making the ultimate sacrifice.

The decision tormented him. How could he, a father who loved his daughter more than anything, condemn her to such a fate? But as the days passed and the destruction worsened, Laomedon knew that he could no longer avoid the inevitable. The gods demanded a sacrifice, and Hesione was the only one who could save Troy.

He summoned his advisors, his voice heavy with resignation. "The sea monster must be appeased," he said, the words tasting bitter in his mouth. "The gods have left us no choice. Hesione... my daughter... must be sacrificed."

The advisors, though horrified, understood the gravity of the situation. They nodded in solemn agreement, though their eyes were filled with pity for their king. The preparations were made swiftly, the people of Troy watching in stunned silence as the news spread. Hesione would be taken to the shore, bound to the rocks as an offering to the monster that had terrorised them for so long.

When Laomedon told Hesione of her fate, she did not cry out or beg for mercy. She simply looked at her father with eyes full of sorrow and acceptance. "If this is what must be done to save our people, then I will do it," she said quietly, her voice steady despite the fear she must have felt.

Laomedon could only nod, his throat too tight with emotion to speak. He wanted to hold her, to tell her that he would find another way, but he knew that there was no other way. The gods had forced his hand.

The day of the sacrifice arrived, and the city of Troy was enveloped in a heavy silence. The people gathered along the shoreline, their faces pale with grief and fear. Hesione, dressed in white, was led to the rocks where she would be bound. Laomedon walked beside her, his heart breaking with each step. The sea churned ominously, as if in anticipation of what was to come.

As Hesione was tied to the rocks, Laomedon turned away, unable to watch. He had lost so much—his pride, his power, his people's trust—and now he was about to lose the one thing he had left. The sky darkened, and the sea monster's roar echoed across the water, sending shivers down the spines of those who heard it. The beast was coming to claim its sacrifice.

But just as all hope seemed lost, a new sound pierced the air—the steady beat of hooves against the ground. The people turned, and there, riding towards them with a confidence that defied the despair surrounding them, was a figure unlike any they had seen before. Clad in the skin of a lion, his muscles rippling with power, he carried a club in one hand and a bow slung across his back. This was Heracles—known to the Romans as Hercules—a hero of unmatched strength and courage.

Heracles dismounted and strode towards Laomedon, his presence commanding attention. "I have heard of your plight, King Laomedon," he said, his voice deep and resonant. "And I have come to offer my help. I will slay the sea monster and save your daughter, but in return, you must promise me a reward."

Laomedon, desperate for any chance to save Hesione, agreed without hesitation. "Anything you ask, it will be yours," he vowed, clutching at this sudden glimmer of hope.

Heracles nodded, satisfied with the king's promise. He approached the shore where Hesione was bound, her eyes wide with a mix of fear and hope. "Do not be afraid," he said gently as he began to untie her. "You will not die today."

As the last rope fell away, the sea monster burst from the water, its monstrous form towering over the shoreline. The crowd gasped in terror, but Heracles stood firm. He picked up his bow, nocked an arrow, and took aim at the beast. With a single, focused breath, he let the arrow fly. It struck the monster between the eyes, and with a final, ear-splitting roar, the creature collapsed into the sea, dead.

The people of Troy erupted into cheers, their despair replaced by joyous disbelief. Heracles had done the impossible—he had saved their city and their princess. Laomedon rushed to Hesione, pulling her into his arms, his heart overflowing with relief and gratitude. But as he held his daughter close, his thoughts turned to the promise he had made.

Heracles approached the king, a faint smile on his lips. "The monster is dead, and your daughter is safe. Now, King Laomedon, it is time for you to fulfil your end of the bargain."

But as Heracles spoke, Laomedon's old arrogance began to resurface. The crisis had passed, the threat was gone, and with it, the fear that had driven him to desperation. The power and security of Troy's walls seemed to restore his sense of invincibility. He looked at Heracles, and for a moment, hesitated. Did he really need to honour this promise, now that the danger had passed?

In that instant, Laomedon made a fateful decision, one that would set the stage for his ultimate downfall.

# LAOMEDON'S SECOND BETRAYAL: THE BROKEN PROMISE TO HERACLES:

The city of Troy had been saved. The sea monster, Poseidon's instrument of vengeance, lay dead beneath the waves, and Hesione, the beloved daughter of Laomedon, had been spared from a terrible fate. The people of Troy, who had only moments before been steeped in despair, now celebrated wildly. Songs filled the streets, children danced, and for the first time in what felt like an eternity, the city breathed a collective sigh of relief.

At the heart of it all stood Laomedon, clutching his daughter close as if he could never let her go again. Heracles, the hero who had done the impossible, stood nearby, watching the joyous reunion with a quiet satisfaction. His presence was as solid and unyielding as the walls of Troy itself, and though he remained still, there was a sense of latent power about him, as though at any moment he could summon the strength that had felled the sea monster.

Laomedon, his emotions still raw from the fear of losing Hesione, turned to Heracles. "You have saved my daughter and my city," the king said, his voice thick with gratitude. "For this, I will forever be in your debt."

Heracles nodded, but there was no need for grand words of thanks. "The reward you promised," he reminded Laomedon, his tone calm but firm. "I do not seek riches beyond what we agreed—only what is owed to me."

Laomedon's heart skipped a beat. In the chaos and terror, he had promised Heracles whatever he desired in exchange for saving Hesione's life. But now, with the immediate danger gone, the king's mind turned inward. The vaults of Troy were not endless, and the toll of the city's recent struggles weighed heavily on him. The sea monster had ravaged the coast, the plague had drained resources, and the city had only just begun to rebuild itself. How could he afford to give away a significant portion of Troy's wealth when his own kingdom still stood on shaky ground?

A flicker of arrogance sparked once again within Laomedon, the same arrogance that had led him to believe he could deceive the gods. The monster was dead, the people were safe, and now, Heracles—though formidable—was just a man. A mortal. What could he do if Laomedon chose not to fulfil his promise?

The thought of reneging on the deal solidified in the king's mind. Heracles had already completed his task; there was no longer any need to fear him. Troy was invincible once more, and Laomedon, as its ruler, was untouchable.

A smile, forced and thin, spread across Laomedon's lips. "Heracles," he began, his voice taking on the smooth, measured tone of a politician, "the city is in a precarious state. The damage to our coast, the lives lost in the plague—it has taken a toll. Surely you, as a man of great strength and wisdom, can understand that Troy cannot spare what you ask for at this time."

Heracles narrowed his eyes slightly but remained silent, allowing the king to continue.

"I would gladly reward you as you deserve," Laomedon added, "but I ask for your patience. When the city has recovered, I will ensure you receive the reward I promised. But now is not the time."

The air grew tense, the celebration around them fading into the background. Heracles stared at Laomedon, and for a long moment, the two men stood in silence, the weight of the king's words hanging between them. Laomedon felt the pressure of Heracles' gaze, but he held his ground, convinced that the hero would accept his excuses and move on.

But Heracles was no fool. He had seen this kind of deceit before, in kings and rulers who believed they could manipulate others with their honeyed words. He had sensed the shift in Laomedon's demeanour the moment the monster was slain, and now, he knew with certainty that the king had no intention of honouring his word.

"I see," Heracles finally said, his voice low and dangerous. "You would betray me, just as you betrayed the gods."

Laomedon bristled, his face flushing with anger. "Betray? You misunderstand me, Heracles. I simply ask for time."

But Heracles had heard enough. He had faced gods, monsters, and challenges beyond the comprehension of ordinary men. Yet here stood a king, puffed up with his own importance, thinking he could deceive a hero who had given everything to save his city. Heracles' patience, stretched thin by the trials he had faced in his life, snapped.

"Your time," Heracles said, his voice rising, "has run out."

Laomedon's heart raced. Heracles' eyes were filled with a fury that Laomedon had not anticipated. The hero took a step forward, his imposing frame towering over the king. "You dare to lie to me? After I saved your daughter from certain death? After I saved your city from destruction?"

The crowd, sensing the shift in the air, began to draw back. The joy of the moment was replaced with fear, as the people of Troy realised that their king had made a grave mistake. Heracles, the hero who had saved them, was not a man to be trifled with.

Laomedon, for all his bluster, felt a tremor of fear pass through him, but still, he could not bring himself to back down. "You are nothing but a mercenary, Heracles," he spat, his arrogance clouding his better judgment. "You were paid with glory. That is reward enough."

Heracles' face hardened, his expression now one of pure resolve. "Then you leave me no choice," he said.

Without another word, Heracles turned and left the city, but the tension that remained in his wake was palpable. Laomedon, watching him go, felt a hollow sense of victory. He had won the argument, but deep down, he knew that this was not the end.

# THE CONSEQUENCES
# OF BETRAYAL:

Heracles did not forget Laomedon's treachery. Betrayal, once tasted, leaves a bitterness that lingers, and the hero's pride had been wounded. Not only had Laomedon broken his promise, but he had insulted the very honour of the man who had saved his daughter's life. It was an offence that could not go unanswered.

Laomedon, blind to the danger he had invited, returned to the business of ruling Troy. He believed that the matter was behind him, that Heracles would move on, just another figure in the long line of those who had come and gone from his court. But the people of Troy, who had witnessed their king's deceit, were not so certain. They had seen the anger in Heracles' eyes, and they knew that men like him did not take betrayal lightly.

Months passed, and the city continued to rebuild itself. But the tension never fully dissipated. It lingered in the air, a constant reminder of the broken promise. Laomedon's advisors, though loyal, began to murmur among themselves, worried about the consequences of their king's actions. And Laomedon, for all his bravado, could not shake the feeling that something terrible was on the horizon.

That terrible something arrived in the form of Heracles, who returned not as a hero, but as a conqueror. This time, he did not come alone. He brought an army, and with it, the promise of revenge. Laomedon's betrayal had cost him not only the loyalty of a hero but the safety of his entire city. The walls of Troy, once thought to be invincible, now stood as a testament to the king's arrogance.

Heracles and his forces laid siege to Troy, and though the city's walls were strong, they could not hold forever. One by one, the defences crumbled, and the city that had once been saved by a hero was now on the brink of ruin because of a king's greed.

Laomedon, trapped within his own fortress, watched as his city fell around him. The very walls he had built with such pride now seemed like a prison, closing in on him as the consequences of his actions caught up with him. Heracles, unstoppable in his fury, breached the gates of Troy and stormed the palace.

When Heracles found Laomedon, there was no mercy left in his heart. The king, once so arrogant, now faced the full weight of his broken promise. And in that moment,

Laomedon realised that the price of betrayal was far greater than he had ever imagined.

# THE FALL OF LAOMEDON: HERACLES 'REVENGE

Time passed after Laomedon's betrayal of Heracles, but the shadow of his broken promise never lifted. Though the city of Troy had temporarily returned to a semblance of normalcy, the tension within its walls remained palpable. Laomedon continued to rule with the same pride that had once driven him to build his mighty city, yet there was an undeniable crack in the foundation of his authority.

He could feel it, even if he refused to acknowledge it—something in the air, in the whispers of his people, in the way his advisors now hesitated before speaking. The calm before the storm.

Heracles had not forgotten. He was a hero forged in the fires of betrayal, a man who had faced challenges from both gods and mortals, and whose strength was matched only by his unyielding sense of honour. Laomedon's insult was not just a slight—it was a wound to Heracles' pride and a stain on his reputation. The promise of vengeance had been sealed in that moment on Troy's shores, when Laomedon had refused to pay what was owed, and Heracles had vowed that he would return.

When the news reached Laomedon that Heracles was approaching, it was not with the quiet tread of a lone hero, but with the thunder of an army at his back. Heracles had gathered his allies, men who were loyal to him, and who saw in his quest for vengeance a righteous cause. Among them was Telamon, his closest companion, a warrior whose strength and loyalty were second only to Heracles himself. Together, they marched on Troy with a force that could not be ignored.

Laomedon's advisors were the first to sense the gravity of the situation. They gathered in the throne room, their faces pale with fear as they urged the king to prepare for war. But Laomedon, ever proud, dismissed their warnings. He stood before them, defiant as ever, convinced that the walls of Troy would hold. "Let Heracles come," he said, his voice filled with the same arrogance that had led him down this path. "Troy is impregnable. No man, not even Heracles, can breach these walls."

But the advisors, more attuned to the growing discontent among the people, knew that Troy was not as invincible as Laomedon believed. The walls were strong, yes, but the spirit of the city had been weakened by Laomedon's deceit. The people, once loyal to their king, now harboured doubts. And doubt, like a crack in a stone wall, could spread and bring down even the mightiest of fortresses.

Heracles and his army arrived at Troy under the cover of night. The moon hung low in the sky, casting a silvery glow over the city's imposing walls. Heracles stood at the foot of those walls, his heart filled with the fire of righteous anger.

He remembered the moment Laomedon had betrayed him, the arrogance in the king's eyes, the way he had dismissed Heracles as nothing more than a mercenary. That insult had festered within him, and now, it would be repaid.

The siege began the next morning. Heracles, with his indomitable strength, led the charge. The city's gates, once thought impenetrable, shuddered under the weight of his blows. The defenders, though brave, could not match the fury of the hero. Heracles fought with the force of a man wronged, his club smashing through stone and iron as if it were mere wood. The walls that had stood so tall now seemed fragile in the face of his wrath.

Inside the city, Laomedon watched from the safety of his palace. At first, he clung to the belief that Troy's defences would hold. But as the hours passed and the sounds of battle grew closer, a cold realisation began to creep into his heart. The walls were falling. His city—his mighty, impenetrable city—was crumbling before his eyes.

The people of Troy, sensing the inevitable, began to turn on their king. Laomedon had betrayed the gods, betrayed Heracles, and now it was they who would pay the price. The streets were filled with panic as citizens tried to flee the coming storm, but there was nowhere to go. The walls that had once protected them now trapped them inside.

Heracles breached the city gates just as the sun reached its zenith, casting a blinding light over the battlefield. The defenders of Troy, exhausted and demoralised, could no longer hold back the tide. Heracles, with Telamon at his side, stormed the palace, cutting through the last of Laomedon's loyal soldiers with ease.

Laomedon, who had once stood so tall and proud, now cowered in his throne room. The walls of the palace felt smaller than ever, the grand columns and tapestries mere shadows of the power he had once wielded. When Heracles entered the room, there was no longer any trace of mercy in the hero's eyes.

"You brought this upon yourself," Heracles said, his voice cold and unwavering. "I gave you a chance to honour your word, to do what was right. And you chose betrayal."

Laomedon, still clinging to the last vestiges of his pride, tried to speak, but the words faltered in his throat. He had nothing left. No excuses, no defences. The king who had once believed himself untouchable now stood face to face with the man whose honour he had scorned.

Heracles did not hesitate. With a single, swift stroke of his sword, he ended Laomedon's reign. The king of Troy, who had built his city on lies and arrogance, fell before the very walls he had once thought would make him invincible.

# THE AFTERMATH

With Laomedon's death, the city of Troy fell into chaos. The people, leaderless and terrified, feared that Heracles would destroy the city entirely. But Heracles was not a man of senseless violence. His vengeance had been exacted upon Laomedon, and with the king dead, his anger began to subside. Troy had suffered enough under the weight of Laomedon's sins.

As the smoke cleared and the city began to quiet, Heracles turned his attention to Laomedon's sons. Among them was Priam, a young man who had witnessed the rise and fall of his father's reign. Priam had always been different from Laomedon—he was kinder, wiser, more in tune with the needs of the people. And though he was devastated by the loss of his father, Priam understood that Troy's future now rested in his hands.

Heracles, recognising something noble in Priam, spared the young prince. He saw in him the potential for redemption, for rebuilding Troy into something greater than it had been under Laomedon's rule. "Your father's mistakes need not be your own," Heracles said to Priam before leaving the city. "Troy can rise again, but only if you learn from his failings."

Priam, humbled and filled with a newfound sense of responsibility, vowed to rebuild Troy—not just its walls, but its spirit. Under his leadership, the city would grow stronger, more just, and more honourable than it had ever been under Laomedon. And so, the young prince began the long, arduous task of restoring Troy, brick by brick, life by life.

In time, Priam would become the greatest king Troy had ever known, a leader who would guide his people through peace and prosperity. But the shadow of his father's betrayal would always linger, a reminder of the price of arrogance and the fragility of power.

Troy would rise again, but the lessons of Laomedon's fall would never be forgotten.

# THE LEGACY OF LAOMEDON: REFLECTION ON HIS REIGN

As the dust settled and the echoes of battle faded, Troy stood once again, battered but unbroken. The walls that had once been Laomedon's pride still towered over the city, their imposing strength a stark contrast to the fragile spirit of the people within. Laomedon, the man who had envisioned those walls as an unassailable barrier against the world, was now gone—his body laid to rest in the ruins of his own ambitions. But his legacy, for better or worse, would endure.

In the days following the fall of Troy, those who had lived through Laomedon's reign began to speak of the king with a mixture of awe and bitterness. He had been a ruler who dared to dream of greatness, who sought to raise Troy to heights never before imagined. The walls that encircled the city were a testament to that vision—strong, magnificent, built with the help of the gods themselves. Under Laomedon's rule, Troy had indeed become a city to be feared and admired across the ancient world.

But Laomedon's legacy was not one of triumph alone. His contributions to Troy's infrastructure, the very stone and mortar of the city, could not erase the deeper scars he had left on its people. For all the physical strength he had bestowed upon Troy, Laomedon had failed in the most important aspect of leadership—honesty, trust, and humility. His reign was marked not just by the construction of walls, but by the lies and betrayals that would come to define him.

The people of Troy remembered Laomedon as the king who had broken promises—not only to the gods but also to those who had trusted him most. His betrayal of Poseidon and Apollo had brought devastation upon the city, and his arrogance in dealing with Heracles had nearly led to its complete destruction. For many, the walls of Troy became a symbol not just of protection, but of the king's hubris—a reminder that even the strongest defences could not save a city from the consequences of its ruler's failings.

As the stories of Laomedon's life were told and retold in the streets and markets of Troy, a clear picture emerged: Laomedon had been a king who sought to make Troy great, but in doing so, he had nearly doomed it. His ambition had blinded him to the importance of integrity and the need to honour his word. His pride had driven him to believe that he could outsmart even the gods, and his greed had led him to betray the very hero who had saved his daughter's life. In the end, it was not an army that had brought Laomedon down—it was his own inability to recognise his limits.

Yet, even in death, Laomedon's legacy was not entirely one of failure. He had laid the groundwork for a city that would rise again. The walls he had built, though now stained with the memory of betrayal, still stood strong. And within those walls, a new leader would emerge—his son, Priam.

# THE RISE OF PRIAM: A NEW BEGINNING

Priam was everything Laomedon had not been. Where Laomedon had ruled with arrogance and deceit, Priam led with humility and wisdom. As a young man, he had watched his father's rise and fall, witnessing firsthand the consequences of pride and dishonesty. Those lessons, painful though they were, had shaped him into a ruler who understood the true nature of leadership. He knew that a city was not built on stone and walls alone—it was built on trust, on the loyalty of its people, and on the respect of its allies.

In the years that followed Laomedon's death, Priam set about rebuilding Troy, not just physically, but spiritually. He sought to mend the wounds his father had inflicted, restoring the city's honour and forging new alliances. Under his rule, Troy flourished once more, becoming a beacon of culture and strength in the ancient world. Priam's leadership was marked by a deep understanding of the fragility of power—he knew that even the mightiest walls could crumble if the foundation of trust was not secure.

But even as Troy thrived under Priam's wise and just rule, the shadow of Laomedon's actions continued to loom over the city. The betrayals of the past had set in motion forces that could not easily be undone. The gods, though appeased for now, had long memories, and the seeds of conflict that Laomedon had sown would one day bear bitter fruit.

# THE EARLY LIFE OF PRIAM AND ASCENSION TO THE THRONE

Priam was born into a world already shaped by the towering shadow of his father, Laomedon, a king whose ambitions and pride had built the magnificent walls of Troy—but whose arrogance had sown the seeds of its near destruction. As the youngest of Laomedon's many children, Priam was never meant to be king. His early years were spent in the shadow of older brothers who were more favoured by their father, destined for leadership. Yet even as a boy, Priam saw things with a clarity and wisdom that set him apart.

Growing up in the palace of Troy, Priam was constantly reminded of his father's power. The grandeur of the city's walls, reaching toward the heavens, filled the boy with awe, but also with a strange sense of unease. His father often boasted of the city's impenetrable defences, built with the help of the gods themselves. But Priam, even as a child, had witnessed the unease and whispers of his father's advisors, the fear behind their eyes whenever Laomedon spoke too loudly of the gods and their debts.

Priam had heard the stories of his father's betrayal—how Laomedon had promised payment to Poseidon and Apollo for their aid in constructing Troy's walls and had then, in his arrogance, refused to honour that promise. He had seen the stormy eyes of Poseidon in his dreams, felt the distant tremors of an anger that was both divine and dangerous. Even as a boy, he understood that promises made to the gods could not be so easily broken.

But it wasn't until the fateful day of Heracles' return that Priam came to understand the full weight of his father's folly. Priam was young when Heracles arrived at the gates of Troy, seeking revenge for Laomedon's second betrayal—the king's refusal to reward Heracles for saving his daughter, Hesione, from the sea monster that Poseidon had sent to destroy Troy. The city trembled with fear as Heracles' army laid siege to the walls, and the boy Priam watched in silent horror as his father, defiant and proud to the end, believed the walls would hold.

Heracles was no mere mortal—his strength was legendary, his anger righteous. Priam could see it in the distance, the way Heracles and his army moved with a purpose that was unstoppable. The walls that had been the pride of Troy began to crumble, stone by stone, under the force of the hero's assault. The city fell into chaos. Priam watched as his father's arrogance was met with divine justice. The city burned, and the cries of his people echoed in his ears as Heracles breached the palace and confronted Laomedon.

Priam never forgot the moment his father fell. It was not just the sight of his father's death that imprinted itself on his memory, but the expression on Laomedon's face—one of disbelief, even as Heracles struck him down. It was the look of a man who had spent his life believing himself untouchable, only to realise too late that he had been wrong. Priam, hidden away in the shadows of the palace, felt something shift inside him that day. He understood, in that moment, that a king's power was not in his walls, nor in his wealth, but in his ability to honour his promises, to earn the trust of his people and the respect of those around him.

# BECOMING KING OF TROY

In the aftermath of Laomedon's death, Troy was a city in ruins. The once-mighty walls had been breached, the palace ransacked, and the people left leaderless. Many of Priam's older brothers had been killed in Heracles' siege, and those who remained were too broken by the events to take up the mantle of leadership. It was in this chaotic vacuum that Priam, the youngest and least expected to rule, found himself thrust into a role he had never imagined.

The people of Troy, still reeling from the destruction, looked to Priam with a mix of hope and desperation. He was young, barely out of boyhood, but there was something in his eyes—something different from his father. Where Laomedon had been proud and distant, Priam carried himself with a quiet humility, a sense of responsibility that had been forged in the fires of Troy's downfall. He knew the weight of the crown now placed upon his head, and he vowed to himself that he would not repeat his father's mistakes.

But Priam's path as king was not easy. The city of Troy was devastated, both physically and spiritually. The once-great kingdom, known for its strength and beauty, had been brought to its knees by the recklessness of Laomedon's broken promises. Priam's first challenge was rebuilding not just the walls, but the hearts of his people.

His first act as king was to address the people directly. Standing before the ruins of the palace, with the broken walls of Troy behind him, Priam spoke with a voice that carried the weight of both grief and resolve. "We have suffered," he said, "but we will rise again. I will rebuild this city, not with arrogance or deceit, but with honour and integrity. Troy will not be known for its walls alone, but for the strength of its people."

These words, spoken with sincerity and humility, began to restore the people's faith in their new king. Priam wasted no time in setting about the task of rebuilding. He worked alongside his people, not as a distant ruler, but as one of them. He oversaw the reconstruction of the city's defences, ensuring that the walls were rebuilt, not just as a symbol of Troy's strength, but as a testament to the resilience of its people.

But Priam knew that Troy's reputation had been tarnished beyond its borders. Laomedon's treachery had made enemies of gods and men alike. The neighbouring kingdoms, once wary of Troy's power, now saw it as weak and vulnerable. Priam's second great challenge was restoring Troy's standing among these kingdoms, regaining the trust and respect that his father had so carelessly squandered.

To do this, Priam turned to diplomacy, forging new alliances where possible and mending old ones where needed. He reached out to neighbouring kings, offering peace and trade in place of conflict. He worked tirelessly to show that Troy, under his rule, would be a city of honour and integrity, not deceit and arrogance. His efforts paid off. Slowly, the name of Priam began to be spoken with respect, and the city of Troy, though still scarred, began to regain its place in the world.

Through it all, Priam was driven by the memory of his father's downfall. He had seen firsthand what happens when a king rules with pride and dishonesty, and he vowed never to follow that path. Instead, Priam ruled with humility, wisdom, and a deep sense of responsibility to his people. He understood that a king's power came not from the strength of his walls, but from the strength of his character.

In time, Priam's leadership would transform Troy into a city of greatness once more. But the lessons of his youth, the fall of Laomedon, and the devastation of Heracles' siege would remain with him always. Priam knew that Troy's future rested on more than just its walls—it rested on the choices he made as king, and the legacy he would leave for those who followed him.

# PRIAM'S RULE: REBUILDING TROY

When Priam ascended to the throne, Troy lay in ruins, its walls scarred from Heracles' siege, its people still haunted by the destruction wrought by his father, Laomedon. The city had once stood as a beacon of strength and prosperity, but Laomedon's arrogance had left Troy broken and vulnerable, its reputation tarnished by betrayal. Priam inherited not just a crown but a fractured kingdom, and the weight of that responsibility was heavy on his young shoulders.

But unlike his father, Priam approached leadership with humility and wisdom. He understood that the first step in rebuilding Troy was not simply restoring its physical structures, but mending the hearts and minds of its people. They had suffered—many had lost loved ones, homes, and faith in their rulers. Priam made it his mission to restore not only Troy's grandeur but its soul.

Priam walked through the city every day, speaking with the people directly, offering words of comfort, and working alongside them. He did not rule from the lofty heights of the palace, isolated from the reality of his people's suffering. Instead, he made himself present in their lives, showing them that their king was not only a ruler but a servant of the people. He oversaw the reconstruction of Troy's defences, ensuring that the walls were rebuilt stronger than ever. But unlike Laomedon, Priam did not boast of their impenetrability. He understood that walls alone did not make a city safe—trust, unity, and leadership did.

Politically, Priam faced the delicate task of restoring Troy's honour among neighbouring kingdoms. The city's reputation had been badly damaged by Laomedon's deceit—his broken promises to the gods and his betrayal of Heracles had left Troy isolated and mistrusted. Priam, recognising the importance of alliances, reached out to neighbouring rulers, offering peace and trade instead of hostility. He sent envoys with gifts and promises of fair dealings, seeking to rebuild the bridges his father had burned.

Priam's humility and sincerity won over many who had once viewed Troy with suspicion. Slowly but surely, Troy's standing in the region improved. Neighbouring kingdoms began to view Priam not as the arrogant son of Laomedon, but as a leader who had learned from his father's mistakes.

He proved himself as a diplomat and a king of integrity, committed to maintaining the peace and protecting his people through alliances, not conflict.

Under Priam's rule, Troy flourished once again. The city rose from its ashes, more magnificent than before, its people renewed in their faith in their king. But Priam never let the success of his reign cloud his judgment. He carried the lessons of his father's downfall with him always, knowing that the power he wielded as king came not from strength alone, but from his bond with the people and the trust they placed in him.

# PRIAM'S FAMILY AND SONS

As Troy's king, Priam was not only responsible for his kingdom's future, but also for his family—his children, who would carry his legacy into the next generation. His wife, Hecuba, was his steadfast partner, a woman of great strength and wisdom who stood by his side through both triumphs and tragedies. Together, they had many children, each with their own distinct personalities and destinies, but none more significant than Hector, Paris (Alexander), and Cassandra.

Priam's relationship with his children was one of the most complex aspects of his life. He was a king, but he was also a father, and those two roles were often difficult to reconcile. His love for his children was deep and unwavering, but he understood that they would one day play key roles in the future of Troy, and that their actions—especially those of his sons—could shape the fate of the kingdom.

# HECTOR: THE DUTIFUL HEIR

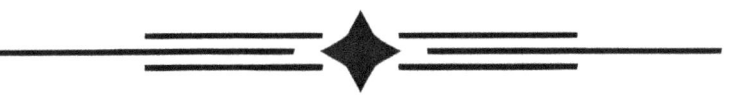

Hector, Priam's eldest son, was everything a king could hope for in a successor. Noble, brave, and fiercely loyal, Hector was not only a great warrior but a compassionate leader. He embodied the best qualities of his father—wisdom, humility, and a deep sense of duty to Troy and its people. Priam saw in Hector the hope of the city's future, a leader who could protect Troy while also guiding it with a steady hand.

Hector and Priam had a bond that went beyond that of father and son. They shared a mutual respect and understanding, often discussing matters of state and war late into the night. Priam trusted Hector implicitly, knowing that when the time came, Hector would be more than capable of taking the throne and continuing the legacy of honourable leadership.

But being the heir to Troy came with great burdens. Hector was constantly aware of the responsibility placed upon him—the weight of the city's safety and its people's hopes resting on his shoulders. Priam understood this, and he often tried to ease that burden, reminding Hector that leadership was not just about battle and strength, but about compassion, wisdom, and the ability to inspire.

# PARIS: THE CHARMING PRINCE WITH A DANGEROUS FATE

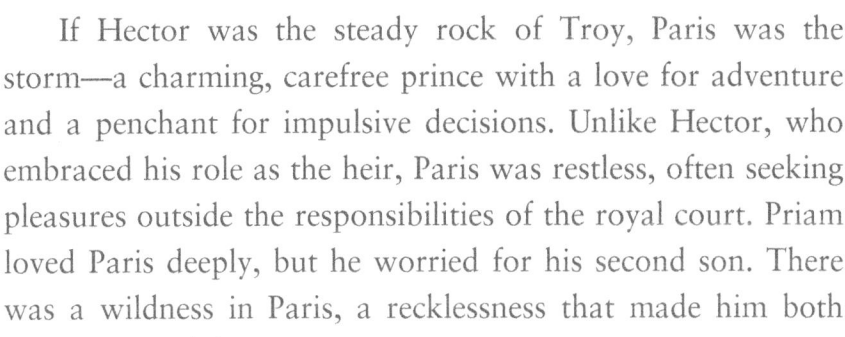

If Hector was the steady rock of Troy, Paris was the storm—a charming, carefree prince with a love for adventure and a penchant for impulsive decisions. Unlike Hector, who embraced his role as the heir, Paris was restless, often seeking pleasures outside the responsibilities of the royal court. Priam loved Paris deeply, but he worried for his second son. There was a wildness in Paris, a recklessness that made him both intriguing and dangerous.

Paris was also the son marked by prophecy. When he was born, a seer had foretold that he would bring ruin to Troy. Horrified by this prediction, Priam and Hecuba had tried to avoid the prophecy by abandoning Paris as a child. Left to die on a mountainside, Paris was rescued by shepherds and raised in the countryside, far from the royal court.

Years later, fate brought Paris back to Troy, and despite the dark prophecy, Priam welcomed his son with open arms. He could not bring himself to reject Paris a second time. He saw the goodness in his son, the same charm that won over everyone he met. But the shadow of the prophecy lingered in Priam's mind, and as Paris grew into adulthood, that shadow only darkened.

When Paris was chosen to judge the contest between the goddesses Aphrodite, Hera, and Athena, Priam felt a familiar unease. The decision Paris made—choosing Aphrodite in exchange for the promise of love—would set in motion events that would ultimately lead to the Trojan War. Paris's abduction of Helen, the most beautiful woman in the world and the wife of Menelaus, king of Sparta, was the spark that ignited the conflict. Priam, despite his love for Paris, knew in his heart that his son's actions had placed Troy in grave danger.

# CASSANDRA: THE CURSED PROPHETESS

Among Priam's daughters, Cassandra stood out not only for her beauty but for her tragic gift—the ability to see the future, a gift given to her by the god Apollo. But Cassandra's gift came with a curse: though she could see the future, no one would ever believe her prophecies. Priam loved Cassandra and valued her intelligence, but he often found it difficult to listen to her warnings, which were filled with ominous predictions about the fall of Troy.

Cassandra's visions of Troy's destruction haunted her, and she often pleaded with Priam and her brothers to take her seriously. But the curse held true—despite her fervent warnings, her words were dismissed as the ramblings of a madwoman. Priam, caught between his love for his daughter and his disbelief in her dire predictions, often struggled to understand the depth of her suffering.

# PRIAM'S STRUGGLES AS A FATHER AND KING

As king, Priam had to make decisions that would impact not only his family but the entire city of Troy. Balancing his love for his children with his responsibilities as a ruler was no easy task. His relationship with Hector was one of trust and mutual respect, but with Paris, it was far more complex. Priam's heart ached with the knowledge that Paris's actions had set in motion events that could lead to Troy's destruction, but he could not bring himself to condemn his son.

Priam's family was his greatest joy and his greatest sorrow. He loved his children with all his heart, but he knew that their destinies, particularly those of Hector and Paris, were intertwined with the fate of Troy. As war loomed on the horizon, Priam understood that the greatest challenge of his reign was yet to come. The choices made by his sons would shape the future of Troy, and as king, Priam could only hope that the wisdom he had imparted to them would guide them in the battles ahead.

## The Prophecy of Paris

From the moment Paris entered the world, his fate was marked by a prophecy of doom. Hecuba, Queen of Troy, had been overjoyed to learn she was expecting another child. But as her pregnancy progressed, her dreams grew dark and foreboding. One night, she dreamt that she gave birth to a burning torch. The flames from the torch spread rapidly, consuming all of Troy, reducing the city to ashes. Hecuba woke in a panic, the image seared into her mind.

She immediately told Priam of her vision. Priam, a man who had seen enough of the gods' whims to be cautious, summoned the city's seer, Aesacus, to interpret the dream.

The seer listened quietly as the queen recounted her nightmare. His face grew pale as he realised its meaning.

"This child," Aesacus warned, "will be the ruin of Troy.

He will bring destruction upon the city and lead to its downfall."

The words fell like a curse over the palace. Priam and Hecuba were horrified. The joy of expecting a new life was suddenly overshadowed by a grim fate. Troy, their beloved city, was to be destroyed by their own child? It seemed inconceivable, but Priam had long learned to respect prophecies. The gods' will could not be easily dismissed, and their warnings had a habit of coming true.

Priam wrestled with what to do. He was not a cruel man, and the thought of abandoning his newborn son filled him with dread. But his love for his city, for his people, was too great. As king, he bore the responsibility of protecting Troy above all else, even if it meant making the hardest decision of his life.

When Paris was born, Priam and Hecuba held him in their arms with a mix of love and sorrow. The infant was beautiful, with a calm, sweet demeanour. He was perfect in every way, making the decision to part from him even more painful. Hecuba wept, but Priam knew they could not ignore the prophecy.

To avoid the curse foretold, Priam and Hecuba made the devastating decision to send Paris away. They could not bring themselves to harm the child directly, but they entrusted him to a servant, instructing him to take the baby to the slopes of Mount Ida, far from the city. There, the servant was to leave Paris exposed to the elements, letting fate take its course. With heavy hearts, they said goodbye to their son, believing it was the only way to protect Troy from the ruin the gods had predicted.

But fate, it seemed, had other plans.

# PARIS'S RETURN AND FATE'S ROLE

The servant left Paris on the slopes of Mount Ida, wrapped in a simple cloth, and walked away without looking back, believing he had done his duty. But the infant did not perish. By chance—or perhaps by the will of the gods—a kind-hearted shepherd named Agelaus discovered the baby lying among the rocks. Moved by the child's helplessness, Agelaus decided to take him in, raising him as his own son in the peaceful, pastoral life of a shepherd.

Paris grew up among the rolling hills and lush valleys of Mount Ida, unaware of his royal lineage. Under the care of Agelaus, he learned the simple joys of life—tending to sheep, wandering the forests, and listening to the soft whispers of the wind through the trees. The beauty of nature surrounded him, and Paris became known for his charm, kindness, and striking looks. To the other villagers, he was just a shepherd's son, but there was always something about him that stood out.

As Paris reached manhood, he began to draw the attention of the spirits and nymphs of the wild. One in particular captured his heart: Oenone, a beautiful water nymph who lived by a stream in the woods. She was ethereal and wise, with the power of healing. Paris and Oenone fell deeply in love, spending their days in the forests, oblivious to the world beyond the mountains. Their love was pure, untouched by the complexities of court life or royal duty. In those moments, Paris was simply a man in love, not a prince destined for tragedy.

But Oenone, with her mystical abilities, could sense that Paris's fate was tied to something much larger and darker than their peaceful life together. In moments of quiet, she would warn him of a shadow she saw in his future—an omen of suffering and betrayal. Oenone, in her love for Paris, told him that no matter what happened, if ever he was wounded or in need, he should return to her, and she would heal him. Paris, smitten with Oenone, promised to stay by her side, never imagining how their lives would change.

The piece of Paris's life on Mount Ida was shattered when the gods intervened, drawing him into a fateful contest. Zeus, king of the gods, had decreed that Paris was to judge a competition between three goddesses—Aphrodite, Hera, and Athena—each vying for the title of the fairest. The goddesses, each offering Paris a bribe for his favour, tempted him with promises of power, wisdom, and love. Paris, captivated by the promise of Aphrodite, who offered him the love of the most beautiful woman in the world, chose her as the victor.

This decision would set in motion the events that would eventually lead to Troy's downfall. The woman Aphrodite had promised Paris was Helen, the queen of Sparta, wife of Menelaus. Paris, unaware of the consequences, was soon pulled from his simple life and thrust back into the world of royal intrigue and power.

It was during a festival that Priam and Hecuba first encountered Paris again, though they did not know it. The young man, now fully grown, participated in a series of athletic contests. His grace and strength were unmistakable, and Priam, watching from the stands, found himself strangely drawn to this shepherd from Mount Ida. Something about the young man reminded him of a son he had lost long ago.

When Agelaus, the shepherd who had raised Paris, saw the recognition in Priam's eyes, he knew the truth could no longer be hidden. He approached the king and queen after the contest, revealing the story of how he had found the infant Paris and raised him as his own. The moment Priam and Hecuba realised that the young man standing before them was their long-lost son, their hearts were filled with both joy and dread. The child they had sent away to avoid the prophecy had returned, and with him, so had the shadow of Troy's destruction.

Despite the prophecy, Priam could not turn his back on Paris a second time. He welcomed his son back into the royal family, hoping that perhaps fate could be avoided after all. Paris was brought to the palace, introduced to his siblings, and given the life he had been denied. But deep in his heart, Priam knew that the prophecy still lingered, and as much as he loved his son, he feared what Paris's return would mean for the future of Troy.

It wasn't long before the events set in motion by Paris's choice in the contest of the goddesses began to unfold. Paris journeyed to Sparta, where he met Helen, the most beautiful woman in the world. Captivated by her beauty, and emboldened by Aphrodite's promise, Paris seduced Helen and brought her back to Troy, triggering the wrath of Menelaus and his brother Agamemnon.

The prophecy that Priam and Hecuba had tried so desperately to avoid was now inescapable. Paris, through his actions, had set in motion the events that would lead to the Trojan War. Fate had intervened, and despite Priam's attempts to protect his city, the seeds of Troy's destruction had been sown by the son he loved but could never fully protect.

# THE ABDUCTION OF HELEN AND THE LEAD-UP TO THE TROJAN WAR PARIS'S JOURNEY TO SPARTA

Paris, now recognised as a prince of Troy, had been swept into a world far different from the pastoral peace of Mount Ida. Surrounded by wealth, power, and courtly expectations, Paris found himself enchanted by the luxuries of his royal life. He had left behind the simplicity of his former days and the love of Oenone, though in his heart, there was always a quiet guilt that haunted him for having abandoned her. Now, emboldened by his newfound status, Paris set his sights on something—or rather, someone—that was destined to bring chaos to the world: Helen of Sparta.

Helen was a name whispered in awe throughout the ancient world, famed not only for her beauty but also for her grace and intelligence. Paris, remembering Aphrodite's promise of the most beautiful woman on earth, felt a pull toward Helen he could not resist. With the goddess's influence swirling in his heart, Paris set out on a diplomatic journey to

Sparta under the guise of forging alliances. But his true purpose was far more dangerous.

When Paris arrived in Sparta, he was welcomed by Menelaus, Helen's husband, who treated him with the hospitality due to a prince of Troy. Menelaus, a straightforward and honourable man, had no reason to suspect Paris's intentions. The palace was grand, the halls filled with the laughter of courtiers and the hum of political conversation, but for Paris, the world around him faded the moment he laid eyes on Helen.

Helen, in turn, was captivated by Paris's charm and beauty. Unlike the stoic Menelaus, Paris was full of life, with an almost boyish sense of adventure and passion. The chemistry between them was undeniable, and it wasn't long before Paris began to seduce her, weaving a romantic fantasy of life in Troy, far from the rigid expectations of her Spartan court.

Days passed, and what began as subtle glances and secret conversations quickly blossomed into a full-blown love affair. Helen, torn between her duties as queen and the intoxicating allure of Paris, found herself ensnared by the excitement he offered. Paris, driven by a mix of genuine affection and Aphrodite's influence, convinced her to leave her life behind and come with him to Troy.

And so, under the cover of night, Helen left Sparta, abandoning her marriage, her kingdom, and her child. She fled with Paris to Troy, a decision that would set the world on fire. As their ship sailed toward the Trojan coast, Helen felt the weight of her choice, the creeping knowledge that there would be no going back. Paris, however, was consumed with a sense of triumph, believing that love had conquered all, blind to the storm that was brewing in their wake.

# PRIAM'S REACTION: LOVE FOR HIS SON VS. DUTY AS KING

When Paris returned to Troy with Helen by his side, it was not the glorious homecoming he had imagined. The court was abuzz with whispers, and the shock of Paris's audacious act rippled through the city. While many admired Helen's beauty, they feared the consequences of what her presence in Troy would mean. This was no ordinary woman—she was the queen of Sparta, and her abduction was a direct insult to Menelaus and the powerful Greek kingdoms.

Priam had hoped that Paris, after being accepted back into the royal family, would grow into a responsible prince who could contribute to Troy's strength and honour. But now, as his son stood before him, presenting Helen as a prize, Priam's heart sank. He could see the fire of youthful love in Paris's eyes, but behind it, he also saw the shadow of the prophecy—the prophecy that had warned of Paris bringing destruction to Troy.

Priam was torn. As a father, his love for Paris was deep and unconditional. He had once feared the worst for his son and had nearly lost him, and the thought of turning against Paris now filled him with sorrow. But as king, Priam knew the gravity of the situation. Paris's actions had crossed a line, and the consequences could be catastrophic. The Greeks would not let this insult go unanswered.

Priam tried to reason with Paris, his voice gentle yet firm. "Do you understand what you've done?" he asked, his eyes searching his son's face for any sign of awareness. "You have taken the wife of Menelaus, a powerful king. This will not end in peace."

But Paris, blinded by love and the belief that Aphrodite was on his side, brushed off his father's concerns. "Helen came with me willingly," Paris said, his voice filled with conviction. "We love each other, and Troy is strong. Let the Greeks come—our walls will hold."

Priam sighed, feeling the weight of both his crown and his fatherly love. He knew Paris was not acting out of malice, but rather out of passion. Still, the decision had been made, and now all of Troy would suffer the consequences. Priam's heart ached, but he could not bring himself to send Helen back or to punish his son. Despite his better judgment, Priam's love for Paris cloud his decision, and he chose to protect his son, even knowing that the price would be high.

# THE DIPLOMATIC FALLOUT

It wasn't long before word of Helen's abduction reached Sparta. Menelaus, humiliated and enraged, wasted no time in gathering his allies. He appealed to his brother Agamemnon, king of Mycenae, one of the most powerful rulers in all of Greece. Agamemnon, always eager for glory and conquest, seized the opportunity to unite the Greek kings under the pretext of retrieving Helen and avenging the insult to his brother's honour. In truth, Agamemnon saw in this conflict a chance to expand his influence and power, and he rallied the might of the Greek forces for a war against Troy.

Before war was declared, however, Menelaus and Agamemnon sent envoys to Troy, demanding Helen's immediate return. The envoys arrived in the city with an air of authority, their message clear: return Helen to Sparta, or face the wrath of Greece. They stood before Priam in the throne room, delivering their ultimatum with cold, calculated words. Priam listened in silence, his heart heavy with the decision that lay before him.

The tension in the palace was palpable. Hector, Priam's eldest son and Troy's greatest warrior, stood by his father's side, his expression grim. He understood the seriousness of the situation better than anyone, and though he loved Paris, he knew that his brother's actions had placed Troy in grave danger. Hector urged his father to consider the consequences, to return Helen and avoid war.

But Priam's heart was torn in two. He knew that returning Helen would be the wise and prudent choice, the one that could possibly avert a catastrophic war. Yet, he could not bring himself to betray his son, the son he had lost once before and had welcomed back with open arms. He looked at Paris, standing defiantly before him, and saw the stubbornness of youth and the blind conviction that love would conquer all.

"I cannot send Helen back," Priam said finally, his voice filled with a quiet resignation. "She is here by choice, and Troy will not cast her out."

The envoys, their patience worn thin, left the palace with grim expressions. War, it seemed, was inevitable. As they departed, Priam felt the weight of his decision press down on him like a heavy stone. He had chosen to protect his son, but in doing so, he had placed his entire city in the path of destruction. The Greeks would come, and Troy would be forced to defend itself against an onslaught unlike any it had ever faced.

# THE LOOMING
# THREAT OF GREECE

As news spread that Menelaus and Agamemnon were raising a great army, the tension in Troy deepened. The people, though loyal to their king, whispered in the streets about the coming war. They knew the Greeks were powerful and numerous, and many feared that Troy would not survive the siege. The walls that had once stood as symbols of their city's invincibility now felt like fragile barriers against the wrath of an entire coalition of Greek forces.

Priam, though outwardly calm, was plagued with doubt. He loved Paris deeply, but he could not ignore the weight of his decision. He spent long hours in the palace, staring out over the city, wondering if there had been another way—if he could have both protected his son and spared Troy from war.

Yet, for all his inner conflict, Priam remained resolute. He could not abandon Paris, not again. The love he had for his son, the same love that had driven him to welcome Paris back after so many years, now bound him to this path. He would protect his family at all costs, even if it meant facing the might of Greece.

In the coming days, as the Greek ships began to gather on the horizon, Priam knew that the prophecy had been fulfilled. Paris had brought Helen to Troy, and with her, the seeds of destruction. The war that loomed would be long and brutal, and Troy, despite its strength, would be tested as never before. Priam could only hope that the love he had chosen to protect would be enough to see them through the storm that was about to descend.

# THE TROJAN WAR BEGINS

# THE SIEGE OF TROY

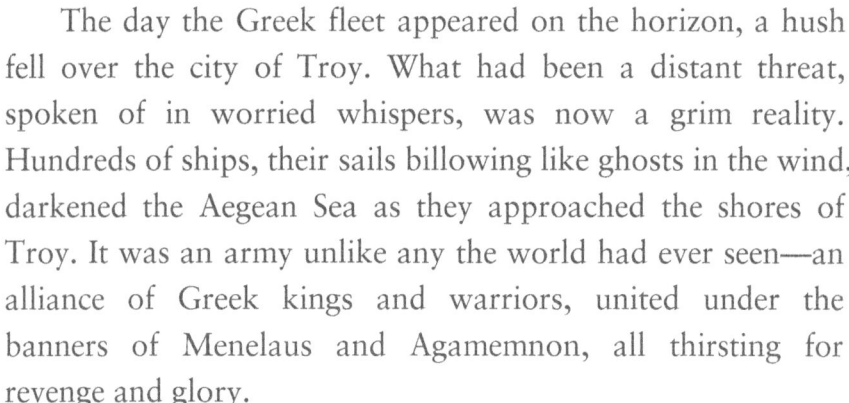

The day the Greek fleet appeared on the horizon, a hush fell over the city of Troy. What had been a distant threat, spoken of in worried whispers, was now a grim reality. Hundreds of ships, their sails billowing like ghosts in the wind, darkened the Aegean Sea as they approached the shores of Troy. It was an army unlike any the world had ever seen—an alliance of Greek kings and warriors, united under the banners of Menelaus and Agamemnon, all thirsting for revenge and glory.

From the highest tower of the palace, Priam watched the ships gather, a sea of war that seemed to stretch endlessly toward the horizon. His heart was heavy with the knowledge that this war, so long in coming, was now upon them. It had been years since Paris had brought Helen to Troy, but the memory of that day, and the fateful choice Priam had made, still haunted him. The love for his son had blinded him to the storm it would unleash, and now Troy stood at the centre of that storm.

As the first Greek warriors disembarked on the beaches, the ground shook beneath their feet. The bronze armour of the invaders glinted in the sun, and their battle cries filled the air. The city of Troy, once a beacon of peace and prosperity, was now a fortress bracing itself for the onslaught of war.

Priam, though an old man by now, knew that the fate of his city rested not in his hands alone. He had raised sons who were fierce warriors, men who would defend their home with everything they had. At the forefront of Troy's defence stood his eldest son, Hector, the pride of the kingdom. Hector was not only a skilled warrior but a leader who commanded the respect of his people and his soldiers alike. Priam knew that Troy's survival depended on Hector's strength and wisdom on the battlefield.

But for Priam, Hector was more than just a warrior—he was his hope, his heart. As king, Priam could not be on the battlefield, but through Hector, he could protect Troy. In the war council, Priam leaned heavily on Hector's advice, listening to his son's strategies and his plans to keep the Greeks at bay. The council was tense, the gravity of the situation hanging over them like a dark cloud, but Priam remained calm, a pillar of strength for his advisors and sons.

"We will not be broken," Priam said, his voice steady as he addressed the council. "Troy has stood for generations, and with the gods' favour, we will stand through this as well."

Hector, though brave, carried the weight of the city's survival on his shoulders. Priam could see the burden in his eyes, but he also saw the resolve there. Hector would not fail him. Together, they planned the defence of the city, fortifying the walls, organising the soldiers, and preparing for a siege that would test every ounce of their strength and endurance.

As the siege began, the city's people looked to Priam for guidance. Though the warriors manned the walls, it was Priam who walked through the streets, speaking with his people, offering words of comfort, reminding them that Troy's walls had held through the ages and would continue to do so. He knew that morale was as important as the strength of their defences, and he made it his mission to show his people that he had not lost faith.

But as the days turned into weeks, and weeks into months, the war ground on, relentless and unforgiving. The Greeks had set up camp on the beaches, their massive force pressing against the walls of Troy in wave after wave of attacks. And though Hector and the Trojan army fought valiantly, pushing back the invaders time and time again, Priam knew that this war would not be over quickly.

# LEADERSHIP DURING THE WAR

Through the long years of the war, Priam remained a figure of dignity and patience. The king, now well into his later years, felt the weight of every decision. The constant threat of destruction loomed over Troy, but Priam never let his people see the weariness in his heart. He met with his advisors daily, listening to reports from the battlefield, discussing strategies, and weighing the options that could prolong their survival. The choices he faced were agonising, but he bore them with quiet resolve.

Privately, however, the war gnawed at Priam's soul. In the silence of his chambers, he reflected on the futility of it all—how a single act of love, or lust, had led to so much death and suffering. He had once thought he could protect his family and his city by standing by Paris, but now he questioned whether that decision had been the right one. As king, he had chosen loyalty to his son, but as the siege dragged on, he wondered if it had been worth the price.

And yet, for all his inner turmoil, Priam never wavered in his duty. He met with the people of Troy regularly, attending ceremonies for the fallen, speaking to families who had lost loved ones, and offering what comfort he could. His presence in the city was a source of strength, and despite the horrors of war, the people of Troy loved and respected him. They saw in Priam a king who was willing to endure alongside them, a ruler who did not distance himself from their pain.

As the years of war stretched on, Priam grew older and more frail, but his resolve never faltered. He remained a symbol of Troy's resilience, a king who, despite knowing the war could only end in tragedy, stood firm until the very end. His role in managing Troy's defence was not one of battle strategy alone, but of preserving the heart of the city—a heart that, even as the walls fell, beat with dignity, honour, and love for his people.

# THE TRAGEDY OF HECTOR'S DEATH

———◆———

The war had raged for years, its endless cycle of violence wearing down both the Greeks and the Trojans. But for the people of Troy, there had always been one unshakable pillar of hope—Hector, the beloved son of Priam and Hecuba, the prince who had stood firm against the might of Greece. He was not only the city's greatest warrior, but also its heart, embodying the strength, courage, and compassion that made Troy endure.

For Priam, Hector was more than just his son; he was the soul of Troy. In Hector, Priam saw the future of his kingdom, a leader who could protect his people and guide them through the darkest of times. As long as Hector lived, Troy had a chance, no matter how dire the situation. But fate, cruel and unrelenting, had other plans.

On that fateful day, the battle outside the walls of Troy took a decisive turn. Achilles, the Greeks' most fearsome warrior, returned to the battlefield, driven by an unquenchable thirst for revenge after the death of his close friend, Patroclus, whom Hector had slain. Achilles, fuelled by a rage that bordered on madness, sought out Hector, knowing that the prince's death would strike the deepest blow to Troy's defences—and to its spirit.

Priam, watching from the palace walls, felt a knot of dread twist in his stomach as he saw Hector, armoured and resolute, step forward to face Achilles. There was no avoiding the fight. Hector, knowing that Achilles was nearly unbeatable, did not shrink from his fate. He carried the weight of his family, his city, and his people on his shoulders, and even as he faced certain death, his courage did not falter.

The duel was brief but brutal, and Priam could do nothing but watch helplessly as his beloved son, his heart, fell to the ground, slain by Achilles' spear. The sound of Hector's body hitting the dust echoed through the walls of Troy like a thunderclap, and in that moment, a wave of unspeakable grief washed over the city.

Priam's legs gave way beneath him. He collapsed, his heart shattered. The shock of it rendered him mute; no tears came at first, just the unbearable silence of loss. Hector was gone—his son, his pride, the protector of Troy. The hope that had sustained the city for so long had been snuffed out, and with it, any illusion that Troy could survive the onslaught.

For the people of Troy, Hector's death was not just the loss of their greatest warrior—it was the loss of their last hope. The streets were filled with mourning, the wails of women and children piercing the air. In the palace, Hecuba's cries rang out, a mother's raw, uncontainable grief. She tore at her garments, inconsolable in the face of the devastating truth: her son, who had fought so bravely for his people, was now dead, his body in the hands of the enemy.

But Priam's grief was different. It was quieter, deeper, like a wound that could not be seen. He had lost many sons in the war, but Hector's death was unlike any other. With Hector's fall, it felt as if a part of Priam had died as well—the part that believed in Troy's future, in the possibility of victory. His heart was broken, and for a long time, he could not speak, could not move. He simply sat in silence, staring into the distance, the weight of his loss too great to bear.

But there was something even more painful than Hector's death: the knowledge that his son's body lay unburied, desecrated by Achilles. In his rage, Achilles had tied Hector's lifeless body to his chariot and dragged it through the dirt, a final act of cruelty that left Priam trembling with both sorrow and anger. To the Trojans, the proper burial of the dead was sacred, a way to honour the lives of those who had passed. But now, Hector's body, once so full of life and strength, was being treated like a trophy of war.

Priam knew he could not let it end this way. No matter the risk, no matter the cost, he had to bring Hector home.

# PRIAM'S JOURNEY TO ACHILLES

In the darkness of night, Priam made a decision that would forever define his legacy. Despite his advanced age and the danger that lay ahead, he resolved to do the unthinkable: he would go to Achilles himself, the man who had killed his son, and beg for Hector's body.

It was an act of both desperation and unimaginable bravery. No king should have to beg, least of all for the body of his son. But Priam, stripped of his royal pride, was not acting as a king—he was a father, and his love for Hector transcended all else. He would risk everything to see his son buried with honour.

Under the cover of night, Priam left the safety of Troy's walls, accompanied only by an elderly servant and a small cart filled with treasures—gifts meant to soften Achilles' heart. The journey to the Greek camp was perilous, but Priam's determination was unwavering. Every step he took brought him closer to the man who had caused him so much pain, but also closer to the possibility of bringing Hector home.

When Priam finally arrived at Achilles' tent, he was weak with exhaustion, but his resolve had not faltered. He entered the tent, and there, sitting by the fire, was Achilles—his son's killer. The two men, so different yet bound together by the cruelty of war, faced each other in silence. For a moment, neither spoke. The air between them was heavy with unspoken grief.

Then, in an act of profound humility, Priam did something no one had expected. He knelt before Achilles, clasping his hands in supplication. "Remember your own father, Achilles," Priam said, his voice breaking with emotion. "For his sake, have pity on me, and return my son."

Achilles, who had been so consumed by rage for so long, was taken aback by the sight of Priam, this great king, kneeling before him. He had never imagined that Priam would come to him in this way, and something in the old man's words stirred a long-buried emotion within him. Priam's plea had cut through Achilles' anger and vengeance, touching something deeper—his own love for his father, Peleus.

For a long moment, Achilles said nothing. But then, slowly, the fire in his eyes softened. He understood Priam's pain in a way that only a son could. Achilles, moved by

Priam's humility and the strength it took for him to come, agreed to return Hector's body.

Priam watched as Achilles ordered Hector's body to be cleaned and prepared for burial. His heart ached as he looked upon his son's lifeless form, but there was also a sense of peace, knowing that Hector would now be laid to rest with dignity. Achilles, in a rare moment of compassion, treated Priam with respect, offering him food and shelter for the night.

The two men, who had stood on opposite sides of a brutal war, shared a meal in silence. For a brief time, they were not king and warrior, but two grieving souls who had lost so much. Priam's bravery and humility in coming to Achilles had shown a side of leadership that transcended the battlefield—he was not only a king, but a father who would go to the ends of the earth for his son.

When Priam returned to Troy with Hector's body, the city wept. The funeral was a somber affair, filled with the sounds of mourning. But there was also a sense of closure, a small solace in knowing that Hector's spirit could now rest. Priam, though shattered by grief, had shown the world the true meaning of love, honour, and sacrifice.

Through his journey to Achilles, Priam had become more than just the king of Troy. He had become a symbol of compassion and strength in the face of unimaginable loss, a leader who, even in his darkest hour, chose humility and courage over pride.

# THE TROJAN HORSE AND THE FALL OF TROY

The war had raged for ten long years. Troy, once a city of unmatched beauty and strength, was now weary. Its walls, though still standing, were worn and battered from countless assaults, and its people, though resilient, had grown tired of the unrelenting siege. Inside the city, there was a growing sense of exhaustion—both physically and emotionally. Priam, now an old man, had seen too much death, too much suffering, and though he kept his head high, the weight of the war was evident in his every step.

It was in this atmosphere of weariness and desperation that the Greeks devised their most cunning plan—the ruse of the Trojan Horse.

After years of fighting, the Greek camp appeared suddenly deserted. One morning, the Trojans awoke to an eerie silence from the battlefield. The Greeks, it seemed, had vanished, leaving behind only a massive wooden horse standing at the gates of the city. The sight of the horse confused the Trojans. There were whispers among the people—had the Greeks finally given up? Was the war truly over? And what could this towering figure mean?

The Trojans, desperate for peace after so many years of bloodshed, gathered at the gates to discuss what to do with the horse. Some believed it was a gift, a symbol of the Greeks' surrender, left as a tribute to the gods in their retreat. Others, more cautious, advised against bringing the horse inside the walls. Among them was Cassandra, Priam's daughter, cursed with the gift of prophecy. She warned that the horse was a trap, her frantic cries cutting through the crowd, but as always, her words were ignored.

Priam, tired and longing for an end to the endless war, allowed himself to believe what he wanted to hear—that the Greeks had finally given up and left for good. He had already lost so much—his sons, his people, and the hope that had once fuelled the city's resilience. In his heart, he yearned for a moment of respite, for Troy to stand in peace once more. The horse, standing tall and silent, seemed to offer that hope.

Against the advice of those who harboured doubts, Priam gave the order for the horse to be brought inside the city. It was paraded through the gates of Troy with great fanfare, the people celebrating what they believed to be their final victory. That night, there was joy and revelry in the streets— something the city had not seen in years. Bonfires were lit, music played, and the Trojans allowed themselves, for a moment, to believe that the war was truly over.

# BUT IT WAS A VICTORY BUILT ON ILLUSION.

As the city slept, unaware of the doom that awaited them, the trap was sprung. Hidden within the hollow belly of the wooden horse were the Greeks' finest warriors, led by Odysseus. Under the cover of darkness, they emerged from the horse, stealthily making their way through the silent streets of Troy. Meanwhile, the rest of the Greek army, which had only pretended to sail away, returned under the shroud of night, creeping back toward the city's unguarded gates.

With the gates thrown open from within, the Greek soldiers flooded into Troy, their pent-up rage and frustration fuelling their attack. The city, caught off guard and defenceless, stood no chance. The sounds of the celebration were quickly drowned out by screams and the clashing of swords. Fires erupted as the Greeks set the city ablaze, their revenge swift and merciless. What had been joy just hours before had turned into a nightmare of death and destruction.

Priam, waking to the chaos, rushed through the palace in disbelief. His city—his beloved Troy—was burning, and there was nothing he could do to stop it. The walls that had stood for generations, the city that had endured for so long, was now falling, piece by piece, flame by flame. Troy, the pride of his reign, was crumbling before his eyes.

# PRIAM'S DEATH

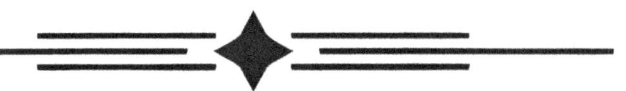

As the Greeks overran the city, slaughtering anyone in their path, Priam, along with his wife Hecuba and several of his daughters, fled to the sanctuary of the Temple of Zeus. In his old age, Priam had lost much of his physical strength, but his dignity and sense of duty as king had never wavered. He sought refuge at the altar, believing that the gods would protect him there. For in Troy, even in the face of war, the gods were sacred, and no man would dare spill blood in their sacred space.

But war does not always respect such rules.

Priam sat at the altar, his hands resting on the cold stone, his thoughts a chaotic mix of grief, guilt, and helplessness.

He had led Troy through ten years of war, but it had all come to this. As he sat in the temple, watching the flames devour the city through the open doors, he reflected on the choices that had led them to this moment. His love for Paris, the decisions made out of loyalty to his family, the war that had consumed them all—it now seemed so distant, so far beyond his control.

But there was no time for long reflection. The Greek warrior Neoptolemus, son of Achilles, stormed into the temple. Unlike his father, who had shown Priam mercy when he begged for Hector's body, Neoptolemus had no pity in his heart. He was driven by bloodlust, eager to continue his father's legacy of destruction.

Priam, still a king in his heart, stood tall in the face of his fate. He met Neoptolemus's eyes, his own gaze filled with defiance and sorrow. There was no begging this time, no attempt to plead for his life. Priam knew what was coming, and he accepted it with the same dignity he had shown throughout his reign.

As Neoptolemus approached, sword in hand, Priam stood firm at the altar of Zeus, his mind not on his own death, but on the city he had loved, the family he had lost, and the era that was now ending. Neoptolemus, without a word, raised his sword and struck down the old king. Priam, the last great king of Troy, fell in the very place where he had sought divine protection. His blood stained the sacred ground, a symbol of the tragic fall of one of the world's greatest cities.

# THE END OF AN ERA

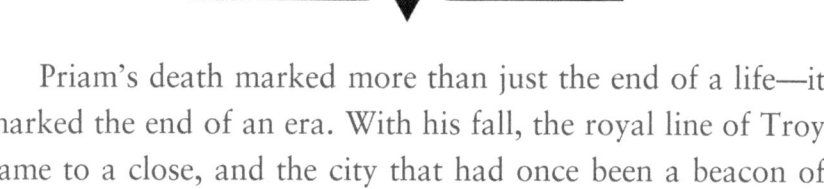

Priam's death marked more than just the end of a life—it marked the end of an era. With his fall, the royal line of Troy came to a close, and the city that had once been a beacon of power and prosperity was reduced to ash and rubble. Priam, who had ruled with wisdom, love, and compassion, had watched helplessly as the forces of fate, prophecy, and war unraveled everything he had built.

In his final moments, Priam did not die as a defeated man. He died with dignity, holding on to the essence of what it meant to be king, even as the world around him crumbled. He had faced impossible choices, losses that no father or king should bear, and yet he had remained true to his people and his family until the very end. His death, at the hands of Neoptolemus, was not just the end of a king—it was the death of Troy itself.

Troy burned, and with it, the legacy of Priam. But in the hearts of those who survived, and in the stories that would be told for generations, Priam's strength, his compassion, and his unwavering sense of duty lived on. He had been a king who embodied the values of leadership not through power, but through love for his people and his family. Even in defeat, Priam had shown the world what it meant to be a king, a father, and a man.

# PRIAM'S LEGACY

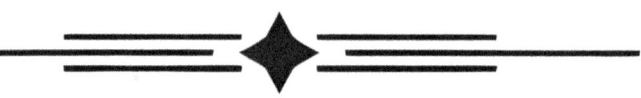

Even as Troy smouldered in ruins, and the cries of the fallen faded into silence, Priam, the last great king of Troy, left behind a legacy that would endure long after the flames had died. Though the city had fallen, reduced to ash and memory, the figure of Priam stood tall in the annals of history, a king who had led with compassion, humility, and unwavering courage through one of the darkest chapters of human conflict. His reign was marked not by victories on the battlefield, but by the depth of his character and the strength he showed in the face of impossible odds.

Priam's legacy began long before the Trojan War, in the way he rebuilt Troy after the ruinous reign of his father, Laomedon. Where Laomedon had ruled with pride and arrogance, Priam governed with wisdom and a deep sense of responsibility to his people. He was a king who understood that a ruler's strength came not from force or deceit, but from the trust and love of those he served. Priam restored Troy, both physically and morally, leading it into a golden age of prosperity and honour. He sought to right the wrongs of the past, mend alliances, and ensure that his people lived in peace and dignity. It was this sense of duty that shaped his entire reign.

But it was during the long, gruelling years of the Trojan War that Priam's true character was revealed. While others were consumed by the violence and bloodlust that defined the conflict, Priam remained a figure of dignity and patience. He watched as war slowly chipped away at the city he loved, yet he never lost sight of what mattered most: his people and his family. Even as the weight of loss mounted, Priam never allowed bitterness or despair to overtake him. He continued to lead with compassion, comforting the grieving, standing beside his people, and ensuring that, even in the midst of destruction, there was still a semblance of humanity in Troy.

Priam's love for his family was one of the defining aspects of his rule. In his children, he saw not only the future of Troy but also the deepest expression of his own hopes and fears. His bond with Hector, in particular, was the heart of his leadership. Hector represented everything that was noble and good about Troy, and Priam's faith in his son was unwavering. The king believed that, through Hector's strength and wisdom, the city could withstand the might of the Greeks.

When Hector fell at the hands of Achilles, it was not just a devastating loss for Troy's defence—it was the breaking of Priam's heart. Yet even in his darkest moment, Priam did not succumb to rage or hatred. Instead, he performed one of the most humbling acts of his reign: he journeyed to Achilles' camp, risking his life to beg for his son's body. Priam, the king of a besieged city, knelt before the man who had killed his son, appealing not to Achilles' sense of honour as a warrior, but to his humanity as a son.

Priam's plea to Achilles was an act of profound humility and bravery. He did not come as a king demanding respect, but as a father mourning his child, a man willing to set aside his pride to give his son the honour of a proper burial. This moment, more than any other, defined Priam's legacy. It showed the world that true leadership was not about holding power over others, but about having the courage to show vulnerability, to love deeply, and to act with compassion, even toward one's enemies.

Priam's humility was not a weakness, but a strength that allowed him to transcend the war and the violence that consumed Troy. While others sought vengeance, Priam sought peace. He understood that his duty as king was not only to protect his people from physical harm but also to preserve their humanity in the face of unimaginable suffering. He refused to let the war strip away the values that defined him and his reign.

Even in defeat, Priam's character stood as a testament to the enduring qualities of true leadership. He was a king who understood that some battles were not won on the battlefield, but in the heart. He faced impossible choices—between his love for his family and his duty as king, between protecting his people and honouring the gods—and yet he did so with grace and courage. Priam's legacy is not one of triumph in war, but of triumph in character.

As Troy burned, as the Greek soldiers sacked the city and the royal line was extinguished, Priam's memory lived on, not as a king who had failed to protect his city, but as a king who had embodied the highest ideals of leadership. His humility, his love for his family, and his courage in the face of impossible decisions became the hallmarks of his legacy.

Priam was the last great king of Troy, but his example endured long after the city's fall. His story, retold by poets and historians for centuries, became a symbol of a king who understood that true strength comes not from wielding power over others, but from knowing when to lay that power aside in the name of love, compassion, and humanity.

In the end, Priam's legacy was not in the walls of Troy, but in the way he lived and led—always with dignity, always with a heart full of love, and always with the courage to face whatever came, even if it meant his own end.

# THE FALL OF TROY AND AENEA'S

# ESCAPE THE SACK OF TROY

The night Troy fell, the air was thick with the acrid smell of smoke and the cries of the dying. Aeneas, like every other Trojan, had fought tirelessly for years to protect his home, but the war had finally reached its brutal conclusion. The Greeks, after ten years of siege, had infiltrated the city through their cruel ruse—the Trojan Horse. From the belly of the massive wooden structure, Greek soldiers emerged in the dead of night, slaughtering the unsuspecting Trojans while their city slept. Aeneas had defended his home with everything he had, but now he stood amid the ruins, watching his beloved city burn.

In the chaos, Aeneas ran through the streets, trying to rally what was left of Troy's forces, though he knew deep down that the city was lost. Flames consumed once-mighty towers, and the sounds of clashing swords filled the air. The Greeks showed no mercy, cutting down men, women, and children alike. Aeneas witnessed horrors no warrior should ever see—the death of his comrades, the slaughter of innocent families, and the destruction of the place he had called home his entire life.

Amid the destruction, Aeneas fought fiercely, his heart heavy with despair but his body driven by instinct. He moved through the carnage with determination, knowing that his survival, and the survival of the few remaining Trojans, depended on him. But there was little hope. The city, Troy, the proud kingdom of his ancestors, was crumbling all around him. Even as he swung his sword in defence, he knew this was the end.

And then, in the heart of this madness, he was stopped— not by a Greek soldier, but by something far more powerful.

# GUIDED BY THE GODS

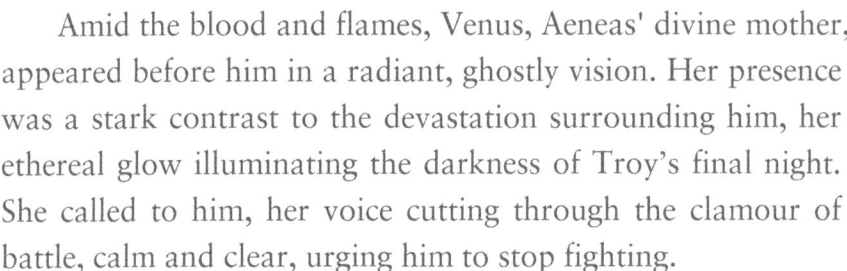

Amid the blood and flames, Venus, Aeneas' divine mother, appeared before him in a radiant, ghostly vision. Her presence was a stark contrast to the devastation surrounding him, her ethereal glow illuminating the darkness of Troy's final night. She called to him, her voice cutting through the clamour of battle, calm and clear, urging him to stop fighting.

"Aeneas, my son," she said, her voice both tender and commanding, "Troy is lost. The gods have decreed it so. But you are not meant to die here. Your destiny lies beyond this city, in a new land, far away from this destruction. You must flee, and you must lead those who remain to safety. A new empire awaits you—this is the will of Jupiter. You cannot save Troy, but you can save its legacy."

Aeneas, still gripping his bloodied sword, wanted to argue, to defy fate, to stay and die alongside his people. But as Venus spoke, he felt the crushing weight of duty fall upon him. He had always known his life was not his own—he was a child of destiny, guided by forces far beyond his understanding. The gods had a plan for him, and no matter how much his heart ached for his homeland, he could not disobey their will.

But how could he leave? How could he abandon everything he had ever known? His ancestors, his friends, the very walls of Troy had shaped him into who he was. To turn his back on all of that now felt like a betrayal, not just to his people, but to himself. The emotional toll was overwhelming. Aeneas looked around at the ruins of his city, the people he loved lost to fire and sword, and he felt a deep, burning sorrow.

Yet he also felt the pull of duty, stronger than ever. He was not just a warrior, he was a leader, and the gods had given him a responsibility he could not refuse. With tears in his eyes and fire in his veins, he nodded to his mother. He would leave. He would take the survivors and fulfil the destiny laid out before him, even if it meant leaving everything he had ever loved behind.

# CARRYING HIS FAMILY AND THE PENATES

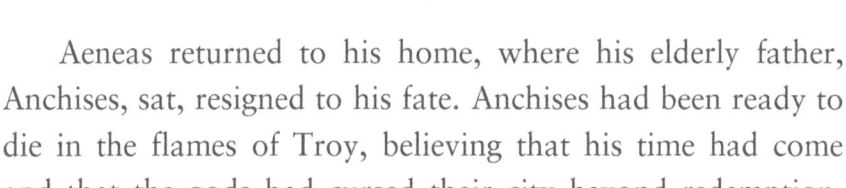

Aeneas returned to his home, where his elderly father, Anchises, sat, resigned to his fate. Anchises had been ready to die in the flames of Troy, believing that his time had come and that the gods had cursed their city beyond redemption. But Aeneas, heart heavy with the weight of the gods' command, could not let that happen. He could not leave his father to die among the ruins.

Anchises, at first, resisted. He was an old man, weary from life, and did not want to burden his son. But Aeneas, with the urgency of fate pressing down upon him, pleaded with his father, and finally, Anchises relented. Aeneas hoisted his father onto his back, a weight that was both physical and symbolic—he was not only carrying his father but also the history and legacy of Troy.

Beside him, Ascanius, his young son, clutched his hand, wide-eyed with fear but trusting in his father's strength.

Aeneas knew that Ascanius was more than just his child—he was the future of Troy, the continuation of its bloodline. Protecting him was paramount.

And then there were the Penates, the sacred relics of the Trojan gods, which Aeneas carried in his other hand. They were the physical embodiment of Troy's spirit, a link to the past that he would carry into the future. Though Troy was burning, its essence would live on, as long as Aeneas kept the Penates safe.

But even as he fled, leading his father and son through the chaos of the city, Creusa, his beloved wife, became separated from them in the confusion. In the panic and smoke, Aeneas called out for her, his heart racing, but she was nowhere to be found. His fear surged as he retraced his steps, searching for her in the ruins, calling her name through the flaming streets, desperate to save her. But it was too late.

Creusa's ghost appeared to him, her face calm, her voice soft as she soothed his frantic heart. "Do not mourn me, my love," she said, her words filling him with both sorrow and strength. "My fate is sealed, but yours is still unwritten. You must go, Aeneas. You must carry our son and our people to safety. A new destiny awaits you, one that I cannot follow. But know this—I will always be with you."

Her words broke Aeneas' heart, but they also gave him the resolve he needed. He could not save Creusa, but he could still save the future she had spoken of—the future that awaited him far beyond the ruins of Troy. With one final glance at the burning city, Aeneas turned away from Troy, the weight of his loss almost unbearable, but his purpose clear.

As dawn broke over the shattered walls of Troy, Aeneas led what remained of his people away from the destruction. He carried his father on his back, his son by his side, and the gods of Troy in his heart. The road ahead was uncertain, fraught with dangers and unknowns, but he knew that the gods had a plan for him. He was no longer just a warrior or a citizen of a fallen city—he was the future of a new empire, destined to build a kingdom that would rise from the ashes of Troy.

But the emotional toll of leaving his home behind weighed heavily on him. Aeneas had lost his wife, his friends, his entire world in one night, and now he carried the responsibility of leading his people to safety. He could not look back, not even for a moment, or he feared the grief would consume him.

As they fled, Aeneas felt the pull of fate, both a burden and a guiding force. He knew that he could not undo the destruction of Troy, but he could carry its spirit forward. With every step, the memories of his home faded behind him, but the vision of what was to come grew stronger. He had lost everything, but the gods had promised him a new beginning.

And so, Aeneas continued, carrying with him not just his family, but the hope of a future yet to be written.

# THE JOURNEY BEGINS: THE QUEST FOR A NEW HOMELAND

# THE SEARCH FOR A NEW TROY

Aeneas stood at the prow of his ship, gazing out at the endless horizon as the wind whipped through his hair. The sea stretched in every direction, vast and unforgiving. Behind him, the ruins of Troy had long since disappeared from view, swallowed by the distance and the weight of his grief. But even as the physical memory of Troy faded, the burden of his people's survival remained. The ships, carrying the last of the Trojan survivors, bobbed in the waves like fragile vessels of hope, yet their course remained uncertain.

Aeneas, with the responsibility of leading the Trojans, could feel the strain with each passing day. The open sea was a relentless force—beautiful in its freedom but treacherous in its unpredictability. The Trojans had set sail with little more than a promise from the gods: that somewhere, in a distant land, Aeneas would found a new city, a new Troy. But where that land was, and how long it would take to find it, remained unknown. Every day, Aeneas watched the faces of his people, saw the weariness etched in their eyes, and wondered how long they could continue this aimless journey.

The sea itself seemed to conspire against them. Juno, ever hostile to the Trojans, had not forgotten her hatred for Aeneas and his prophesied destiny to found a new empire that would one day rival her beloved Carthage. In her anger, she unleashed storm after storm, battering their ships with wind and rain, tossing them like leaves in a tempest. Aeneas stood firm, but each storm took its toll, the sailors fighting against the waves while the refugees clung to each other in fear.

As the days turned to weeks and the weeks to months, the Trojans began to lose hope. They had escaped the flames of Troy only to be cast adrift in an endless ocean, at the mercy of hostile gods and cruel fate. Aeneas himself, though determined, felt the weight of his people's despair. He had promised them a new home, but every day that passed without land on the horizon made that promise feel more distant, more like a dream.

# ENCOUNTERS WITH THE HARPIE

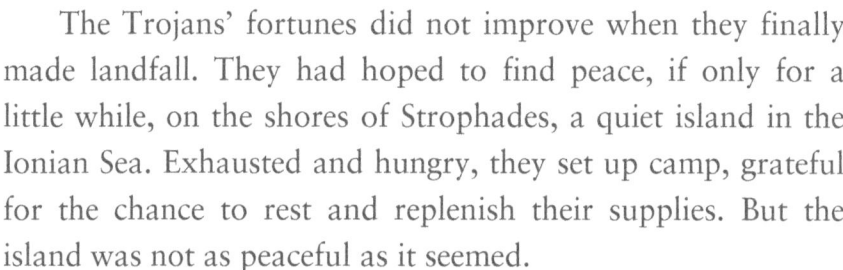

The Trojans' fortunes did not improve when they finally made landfall. They had hoped to find peace, if only for a little while, on the shores of Strophades, a quiet island in the Ionian Sea. Exhausted and hungry, they set up camp, grateful for the chance to rest and replenish their supplies. But the island was not as peaceful as it seemed.

As they gathered food from the island's rich fields, a terrible shriek pierced the air. From the skies descended the Harpies, monstrous creatures with the bodies of birds and the faces of women. Their talons were sharp, their wings black as night, and they swooped down upon the Trojans, tearing at their food and fouling their feast with filth.

Aeneas and his men tried to drive the creatures away, but the Harpies were relentless, attacking with a fury that could not be quelled.

Aeneas, sword in hand, led the charge, but it was no use. The Harpies' strength was unnatural, fuelled by some dark magic, and no matter how many times the Trojans fought them off, the creatures returned, shrieking and cursing.

At last, one of the Harpies, Celaeno, rose above the rest, her voice cutting through the chaos. "You may drive us from our island," she hissed, her eyes gleaming with malice, "but you will never escape our curse! You will wander these seas for years, Aeneas, and when you do find your home, you will be so starved, so desperate, that you will eat your very tables!"

The curse sent a chill through the Trojans. Even as the Harpies retreated into the sky, leaving the island desolate once again, the weight of Celaeno's words lingered like a dark cloud over their hearts. Aeneas, though shaken, knew that this was just one more trial on their long journey, one more test of their endurance. He reminded his people of their destiny, the promise that the gods had made to them, but inside, he too felt the growing fear that their hardships were far from over.

# MEETING KING HELENUS

After weeks of navigating treacherous seas, Aeneas and his people found refuge in the kingdom of Helenus, a Trojan prince who had managed to carve out a small realm in Epirus, far from the reach of the Greeks. For the first time in many months, Aeneas and his companions found themselves in the company of fellow Trojans, greeted not with hostility but with open arms and warmth.

Helenus, a seer gifted with the power of prophecy, welcomed Aeneas like a brother. The two men spoke at length about their shared history and the trials they had endured since the fall of Troy. Helenus, though he had found peace in his new kingdom, knew that his fate was not the same as Aeneas'. He could not leave Epirus, but he could offer Aeneas guidance on the perilous road ahead.

In the quiet chambers of his palace, Helenus revealed the future to Aeneas. "Your journey is far from over," he warned. "The gods will continue to test you, and many dangers lie ahead. But you are destined for Italy, the land where your new city will rise. There, your people will find their new home."

Helenus' prophecy was both comforting and daunting. While it confirmed that Italy was indeed the destination, it also hinted at the challenges that still awaited them.

Helenus spoke of the monsters Scylla and Charybdis, whose waters Aeneas must avoid at all costs. These terrible creatures guarded the narrow straits of Sicily, and to attempt to pass between them would be certain doom.

"Trust the gods," Helenus said, his voice heavy with the wisdom of his prophetic gift. "But also trust yourself. You have the strength to lead your people, no matter what lies ahead."

With Helenus' parting words in his heart, Aeneas prepared to continue the journey, his resolve renewed. Though the seas ahead were treacherous and the trials numerous, he knew that the gods had not abandoned him. His people's destiny was in his hands, and he would not fail them.

# AENEAS 'JOURNEY CONTINUES

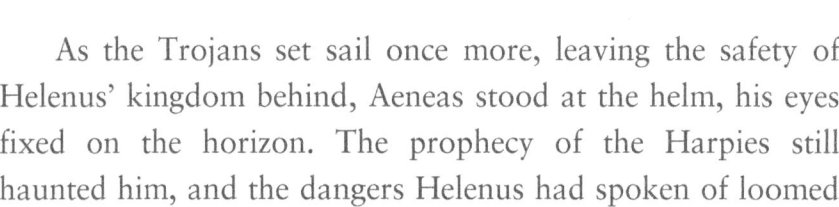

As the Trojans set sail once more, leaving the safety of Helenus' kingdom behind, Aeneas stood at the helm, his eyes fixed on the horizon. The prophecy of the Harpies still haunted him, and the dangers Helenus had spoken of loomed large in his mind. But despite the trials ahead, Aeneas knew that he could not turn back. His people, the last remnants of Troy, looked to him for guidance, and he would carry them forward, through storm, monster, and curse.

The road to Italy was long, but Aeneas had learned one thing above all—his journey was not just about survival. It was about faith. Faith in the gods, faith in his people, and, most importantly, faith in himself. No matter how many obstacles lay between him and his destined land, Aeneas knew that he was the one chosen to guide Troy's legacy to its new home.

# THE ROMANCE WITH DIDO IN CARTHAGE ARRIVAL IN CARTHAGE

After weeks of being tossed by the relentless sea, Aeneas and his weary band of Trojans were at the mercy of the stormy waters once again. The waves roared, and the sky darkened as the storm, sent by the ever-hostile Juno, threatened to destroy them completely. Aeneas, though hardened by years of war and hardship, could do nothing but pray for mercy as the winds battered their ships. But the gods, as ever, had other plans.

As the storm raged, Venus, Aeneas' divine mother, intervened. She could not bear to see her son's journey cut short, and with a gentle plea to Neptune, she calmed the storm, guiding Aeneas' ship to safety. As the clouds parted and the rain ceased, the Trojans found themselves washed up on the shores of Carthage, a burgeoning city in North Africa, ruled by the proud and beautiful Queen Dido.

Upon arrival, Aeneas and his men were exhausted, but they were welcomed warmly by Dido, a woman of great charm and strength. Dido, herself no stranger to sorrow, had fled her homeland after the murder of her husband and founded Carthage on her own. She saw in Aeneas a kindred spirit, a man also exiled from his home and seeking to rebuild. The mutual admiration between them was immediate, and Aeneas, grateful for the hospitality, felt a sense of peace he hadn't known since the fall of Troy.

But their meeting was not left to chance. Juno, ever plotting to divert Aeneas from his destiny, saw an opportunity in Carthage. If Aeneas could be kept here, if he could fall in love with Dido, perhaps he would forget his fate and remain in Carthage, abandoning his mission to found a great empire that would one day rival her beloved Carthage.

With Venus' reluctant cooperation, the gods wove a spell of love around Aeneas and Dido, setting into motion a romance that would change both their fates forever.

# THE LOVE AFFAIR

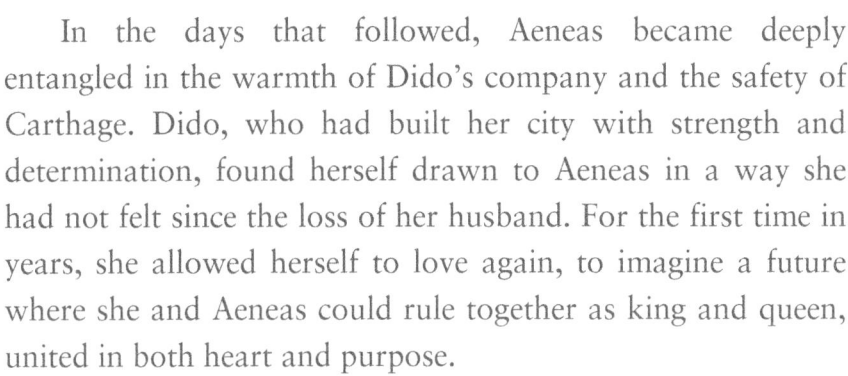

In the days that followed, Aeneas became deeply entangled in the warmth of Dido's company and the safety of Carthage. Dido, who had built her city with strength and determination, found herself drawn to Aeneas in a way she had not felt since the loss of her husband. For the first time in years, she allowed herself to love again, to imagine a future where she and Aeneas could rule together as king and queen, united in both heart and purpose.

Aeneas, too, was captivated. After years of hardship and wandering, Carthage felt like a haven—a place where he could rest, where the weight of destiny seemed, for once, to ease. He and Dido spent their days together, their bond deepening with each passing moment. The Trojans, seeing their leader so content, began to settle into Carthage, helping to build the city and considering it their new home. Aeneas, for the first time since Troy's fall, began to dream of staying, of building a life with Dido.

The days blurred into weeks, and Aeneas, once so driven by the gods' will, seemed to forget his mission. Dido envisioned a future where they would rule side by side, their love not only strengthening Carthage but also securing a powerful future for her people. The two shared long walks through the gardens, meals in the palace, and moments of laughter and intimacy that made the weight of the world seem distant.

But beneath the surface, there was always the faint pull of something unresolved—a reminder, a whisper of a destiny not yet fulfilled. Aeneas, though happy, was never truly free of the responsibility that hung over him. The gods had not forgotten, and neither, deep down, had he.

# JUPITER'S COMMAND

As Aeneas and Dido revelled in their love, the gods looked down with disapproval. Jupiter, the king of the gods, saw that Aeneas was lingering too long in Carthage, abandoning his destiny for the comfort of the present. It was not the future Jupiter had planned for him, and the fate of a great empire—Rome—depended on Aeneas fulfilling his mission. With growing frustration, Jupiter sent Mercury, his swift messenger, to remind Aeneas of his divine purpose.

Mercury appeared before Aeneas one evening, as he stood overlooking the sea, lost in thought. "Aeneas, son of Anchises," Mercury's voice cut through the warm air, urgent and stern, "why do you linger here, forgetting the great destiny that awaits you? The gods have not decreed this land for you. Italy calls, and your empire waits. You must leave this place and fulfil the will of Jupiter. It is not for you to build your future here."

Aeneas' heart sank. He had known this moment would come, but the reality of it still hit him like a wave. How could he leave now, after finding peace in Dido's arms, after beginning to rebuild what he had lost? But he knew, deep in his soul, that Mercury spoke the truth. His destiny was not in Carthage. It was in Italy, and he could not defy the will of the gods. He had a people to lead, a city to found, and a legacy to establish.

With a heavy heart, Aeneas realised what he had to do. He could not stay. He would have to leave Dido, leave the life they had begun to build together, and return to the path laid out for him by fate. The thought of it tore at him, but the weight of his responsibility was too great to ignore.

# DIDO'S DESPAIR AND SUICIDE

That night, Aeneas made his decision. Without a proper farewell, fearing that Dido's pleas would weaken his resolve, he gave the order for the Trojans to prepare their ships. In the darkness, they began to pack their belongings, quietly preparing to sail away under the cover of night. Aeneas stood on the shore, watching as the preparations were made, his heart aching with guilt and sorrow.

Dido, however, soon learned of his departure. She confronted Aeneas in a storm of fury and heartbreak, her voice trembling with betrayal. "How could you leave me like this? After all we've shared? Was it all a lie, Aeneas? Am I nothing more than a momentary distraction to you?" Her grief and rage spilled out in a torrent, her once calm and collected demeanour now shattered by the depth of her love and the pain of her abandonment.

Aeneas, torn between his love for her and his duty, tried to explain. "It is not my will, Dido. It is the will of the gods. My fate lies in Italy—I must go, for the sake of my people, for the sake of the future that awaits me. Please understand, I never wanted to hurt you."

But Dido's heart had already broken. She could not understand how the man she loved could walk away, how the promises they had made could be so easily discarded in the name of fate. Aeneas' words, though sincere, offered her no comfort. As she watched him leave, her despair deepened into something darker, something irreversible.

That night, as the Trojan ships disappeared over the horizon, Dido stood on the cliffs above Carthage, her heart consumed by pain. Unable to bear the weight of her loss, she climbed to the pyre she had built, the fire burning brightly as a symbol of her grief. With one final curse on Aeneas and his descendants, she threw herself onto the flames, her life ending in a tragic blaze of sorrow and betrayal.

Dido's death marked not only the end of a great queen, but the beginning of a bitter enmity between Carthage and Rome, a hatred born of love and broken promises. As Aeneas sailed away, he felt the weight of her death in his heart, knowing that his choices had led to her ruin. But there was no turning back. His path, though fraught with pain, was already written in the stars.

# THE ASCENDING TO
# THE ANCESTORS
# ARRIVAL IN ITALY
# AND THE SIBYL

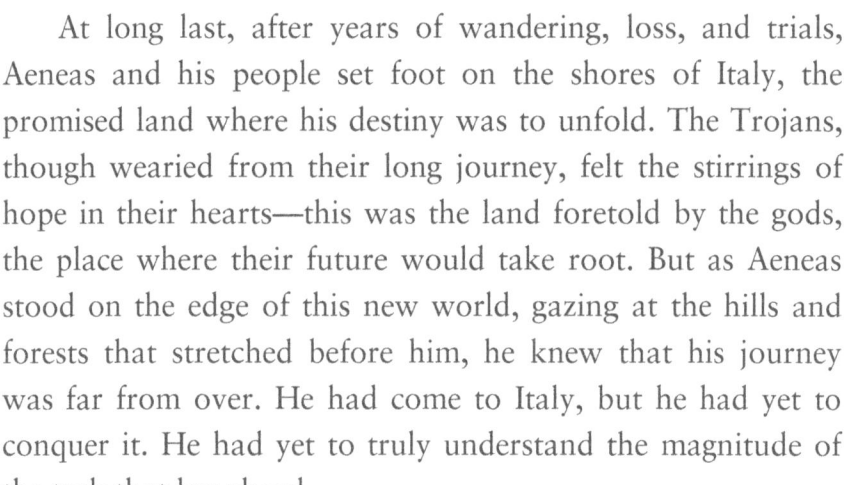

At long last, after years of wandering, loss, and trials, Aeneas and his people set foot on the shores of Italy, the promised land where his destiny was to unfold. The Trojans, though wearied from their long journey, felt the stirrings of hope in their hearts—this was the land foretold by the gods, the place where their future would take root. But as Aeneas stood on the edge of this new world, gazing at the hills and forests that stretched before him, he knew that his journey was far from over. He had come to Italy, but he had yet to conquer it. He had yet to truly understand the magnitude of the task that lay ahead.

Seeking guidance, Aeneas made his way to the sacred site of Cumae, where the renowned Sibyl, a prophetess who communed with the gods, resided. The Sibyl's cave, hidden deep within the rocky cliffs, was a place of ancient power, its walls echoing with the whispers of fate. When Aeneas entered her chamber, the air was heavy with incense, and the flickering light cast strange shadows on the walls. The Sibyl, her eyes glowing with divine insight, greeted him, already aware of his quest.

"You have come far, Aeneas," the Sibyl said, her voice low and resonant. "But the greatest trials still await you. You seek to build a new city, a new Troy, but before you can do so, you must understand the full scope of your destiny. The gods have decreed that you will found a great empire, but to carry the weight of such a task, you must seek out the wisdom of those who came before you. You must ascend into the World of the Ancestors, where the spirits of the dead dwell."

Aeneas felt a shiver pass through him at her words. The thought of entering the realm of the dead, of confronting the spirits of those he had lost, filled him with a sense of awe and dread. Yet, he knew that this journey was necessary. If he was to fulfil his destiny, he had to seek the guidance of his father, Anchises, whose wisdom would light the way forward. The Sibyl led him to the entrance of the portal which looked like a shimmering waterfall, warning him that while the path to the ancestors was filled with peril, it was the only way to truly understand the weight of his fate.

# JOURNEY THROUGH THE WORLD OF THE ANCESTORS

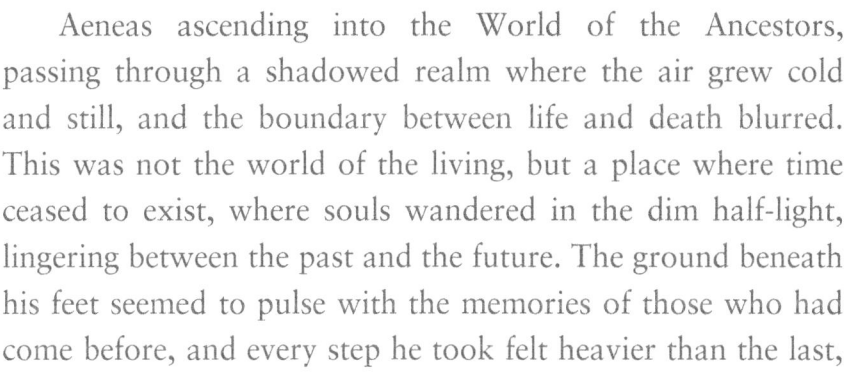

Aeneas ascending into the World of the Ancestors, passing through a shadowed realm where the air grew cold and still, and the boundary between life and death blurred. This was not the world of the living, but a place where time ceased to exist, where souls wandered in the dim half-light, lingering between the past and the future. The ground beneath his feet seemed to pulse with the memories of those who had come before, and every step he took felt heavier than the last,

as if the very air was filled with the weight of ancient sorrow.

As he ventured deeper, Aeneas began to encounter the shades of those he had known in life. Among the first was the figure of Dido, the queen of Carthage, who had loved him deeply and whose heart he had broken when he left her to fulfil his mission. Aeneas felt a pang of guilt as he saw her—her eyes once filled with warmth and love now cold with anger and grief. He called out to her, his voice heavy with remorse, "Dido, it was never my choice to leave you. The gods commanded me to leave, to fulfil my destiny."

But Dido did not speak. She turned away, her silent refusal more painful than any words. Aeneas watched her fade into the shadows, her unspoken curse lingering in the air. He knew that she would never forgive him, and the pain of her loss, of the life they might have shared, would haunt him forever.

Further along the path, Aeneas encountered the spirits of his fallen comrades—warriors from Troy, men who had fought and died by his side, now reduced to pale, flickering memories of their former selves. They greeted him with solemn nods, their faces etched with the silent grief of lives cut short. Each encounter was a reminder of the cost of war, the countless lives sacrificed in the name of destiny. Yet, as he passed through this spectral army, Aeneas felt their unspoken trust in him—they had given their lives believing in the future he would build. He could not fail them now.

At last, Aeneas reached the innermost part of the World of the Ancestors, where the shade of his father, Anchises, awaited him. Anchises stood tall, his face serene, as if untouched by the sorrow that filled this place. The sight of his father filled Aeneas with both relief and longing. He had missed him more than he could express, and yet, there was no time for the comforts of reunion. Anchises, always wise, knew why Aeneas had come.

# ANCHISES 'PROPHECY

"Aeneas, my son," Anchises said, his voice like a gentle breeze from a distant past, "you have come far, but the path ahead is even more treacherous. I have watched over you, and I know the burdens you carry. But now, it is time for you to understand the full weight of your destiny. The future that lies before you is not just for you or your people—it is the future of an entire empire."

Anchises then revealed to Aeneas a vision of what was to come. In the swirling mists of the World of the Ancestors, Aeneas saw the faces of great leaders and heroes—men who would one day shape the world. He saw the rise of Rome, a city greater than Troy, built by the hands of his descendants. He saw the likes of Romulus and Remus, who would found the city, and the great emperors who would lead Rome to glory. He saw battles fought and won, cities built and lost, and the threads of fate that wove them all together in an intricate tapestry. Each thread represented the choices, sacrifices, and victories of Aeneas' future bloodline. The vision was vast, stretching far beyond anything Aeneas had imagined. He saw Augustus, the first emperor of Rome, whose reign would bring peace after years of civil war, and whose legacy would stand as a beacon of Roman greatness.

He saw Julius Caesar, a man whose ambition would both elevate and fracture the republic, leading to the birth of an empire.

Aeneas watched as the empire grew, spreading across the known world, its influence shaping the fate of nations. He saw the construction of grand temples, the rise of vast armies, and the development of laws and cultures that would last for millennia. Rome would not only be a city of power, but of wisdom, art, and civilisation. This empire, Anchises explained, would be the culmination of Aeneas' journey and the reward for his sacrifices.

"Your descendants will be great," Anchises continued, "but greatness comes at a cost. They will face challenges as you do now. War will find them, peace will elude them at times, but in the end, their legacy will endure. The empire they build will stand as a testament to your courage, your endurance, and your willingness to follow the path the gods have laid before you."

Aeneas, awestruck by the vision, felt both a sense of pride and a growing weight on his heart. The future of this great empire depended on him. The lives of his people, the foundation of this eternal city—everything rested on his shoulders. He had already endured so much, but now, with this vision laid bare, he understood that his trials were not simply his own. He carried the hopes and dreams of generations yet unborn.

# THE WEIGHT OF RESPONSIBILITY

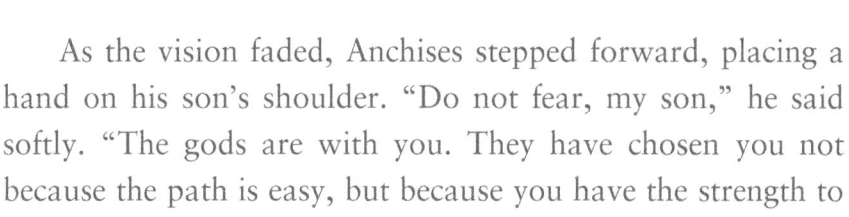

As the vision faded, Anchises stepped forward, placing a hand on his son's shoulder. "Do not fear, my son," he said softly. "The gods are with you. They have chosen you not because the path is easy, but because you have the strength to walk it. You will face battles yet, but never forget that your journey will give rise to a greatness beyond measure. Rome will be the light of the world."

Aeneas, his heart heavy with the knowledge of his future responsibilities, nodded. The reunion with his father had given him clarity, but it had also reminded him of the immense burden he carried. He had not simply been wandering in search of a home—he had been building the foundation for an empire that would stand the test of time. His journey was no longer just about survival; it was about the future of a people and a civilisation that would endure long after his own life had ended.

With Anchises' words ringing in his ears and the vision of Rome's future burned into his memory, Aeneas turned and began his ascent back to the world of the living. His steps were slower, more deliberate, as he reflected on the path ahead. He knew now that his trials were not just personal— they were cosmic, part of a greater plan that would shape the fate of the world.

When Aeneas emerged from the World of the Ancestors, the air felt different—charged with the weight of the responsibility he now carried. He had seen the future, and it had both inspired and burdened him. But despite the heaviness of his heart, there was also a renewed sense of purpose within him. He could not afford to fail. He would build the city, he would fulfil his destiny, and Rome would rise from the ashes of Troy.

Aeneas' journey was far from over, but now, more than ever, he understood its true significance. It was no longer just about finding a new home; it was about building the foundation for an empire that would last forever. The responsibility was immense, but Aeneas had the strength and the will to carry it forward. The future of Rome awaited him.

# CONFLICT IN LATIUM: WAR WITH TURNUS ARRIVAL IN LATIUM

When Aeneas and his weary band of survivors finally set foot on the fertile plains of Latium, it seemed their long search for a new home had come to an end. King Latinus, the wise and venerable ruler of the land, welcomed them with open arms. He had heard whispers from the gods, visions that spoke of a foreign prince destined to marry his daughter, Lavinia, and unite their people in peace. In Aeneas, Latinus saw the fulfilment of this prophecy—a man hardened by loss, yet guided by fate toward a future greater than any he had dreamed of.

For Aeneas, this was a moment of hope. The gods had led him here, to this rich and bountiful land, and now, it seemed his people could finally lay down roots. The possibility of peace, of love, and of a new beginning stood before him. Yet even as he envisioned this future, the seeds of conflict were already being sown.

# TURNUS AND THE WAR

Turnus, the proud and fiery prince of the Rutulians, had long been betrothed to Lavinia. In his eyes, she was rightfully his, and Aeneas' arrival threatened not only his claim to her hand but his very honour. Turnus, once a beloved figure among the local tribes, became consumed by jealousy and rage. His mind seethed with thoughts of betrayal and vengeance. How could a stranger—a Trojan, no less—come and take from him what was promised?

Fueled by his wounded pride, Turnus stirred the hearts of the local tribes, kindling the flames of war. He roused their anger, reminding them of the foreign invaders who now sought to impose themselves upon their land. With every word, Turnus made the coming conflict personal—about more than Lavinia, about defending their heritage, their land, and their pride from outsiders.

The war, like so many others, was born from misunderstanding, jealousy, and the delicate pride of men. For Aeneas, it was a tragic turn of fate. He had come seeking peace and unity, but instead, he was thrust once more into the horrors of battle.

# AENEAS AS A MILITARY LEADER

Aeneas, though weary of war, accepted the call to defend his people. He had seen enough death to last a lifetime, but duty to the Trojans, and the gods who guided him, left him no choice. As the leader of his people, he could not shrink from the conflict. Yet even as he donned his armour, his heart was heavy. He knew that this was not a fight he had sought, and his soul ached at the thought of spilling blood once more.

On the battlefield, Aeneas' leadership shone brightly. He fought with the strength of a man who knew the cost of war but had resolved to protect his people at any price. Under his command, the Trojans fought fiercely, inspired by their leader's courage. Yet, unlike Turnus, Aeneas was not driven by personal vengeance. His mind always turned to the well-being of his people and the land he hoped to make their home. He sought to end battles quickly, to spare lives wherever possible, and to treat his enemies with respect.

Aeneas was no stranger to loss, and that experience had softened him in a way war often failed to do for others. He understood that each soldier who fell had a family, had dreams. Though he fought with valour, he sought peace even in the midst of conflict. His compassion extended beyond his own people—he grieved for the lives lost on both sides, hoping that this war would not stretch beyond necessity.

As the war raged on, Aeneas faced Turnus in battle. He admired Turnus' strength and bravery, though he lamented the fiery pride that had brought them to this point. He did not hate his enemy; rather, he pitied him for being trapped by fate and circumstance, just as he had been.

# THE DEATH OF PALLAS AND AENEA'S RAGE THE DEATH OF PALLAS

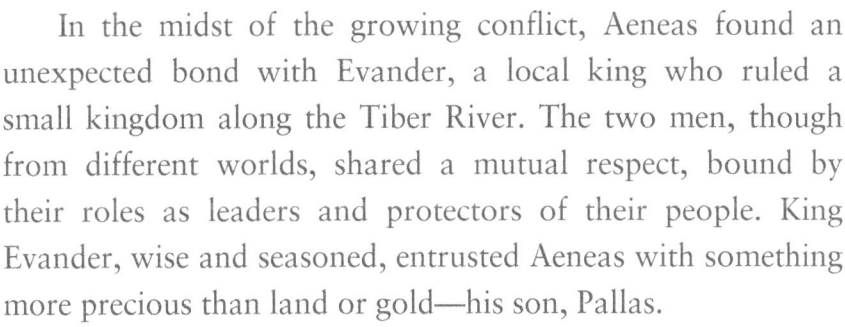

In the midst of the growing conflict, Aeneas found an unexpected bond with Evander, a local king who ruled a small kingdom along the Tiber River. The two men, though from different worlds, shared a mutual respect, bound by their roles as leaders and protectors of their people. King Evander, wise and seasoned, entrusted Aeneas with something more precious than land or gold—his son, Pallas.

Pallas, young and full of promise, had an eager heart and a spirit that sought glory. He looked to Aeneas not just as a leader but as a mentor, seeing in him the strength and wisdom he hoped to emulate. Aeneas, in turn, felt a deep responsibility for the boy, almost as if he were his own son. As they rode into battle, Aeneas saw in Pallas the future of this land—a symbol of hope, the promise of what could be built after the bloodshed had ended.

But war, as Aeneas knew too well, was unforgiving. During a brutal clash with the Rutulians, Pallas fought valiantly, but fate had already marked him for tragedy. Turnus, his heart burning with the desire to prove himself in battle, came face to face with the young warrior. Though Pallas fought with all his might, Turnus struck him down, a victory tainted by the knowledge that it would cost the boy his life.

When Aeneas learned of Pallas' death, the weight of it struck him deeply. He had seen countless friends and comrades fall, but Pallas' death was different. It was personal. He had promised Evander that he would protect his son, and now that promise lay shattered in the dust. The loss pierced him in a way few others had, igniting a deep and burning sorrow.

# AENEAS 'WRATH

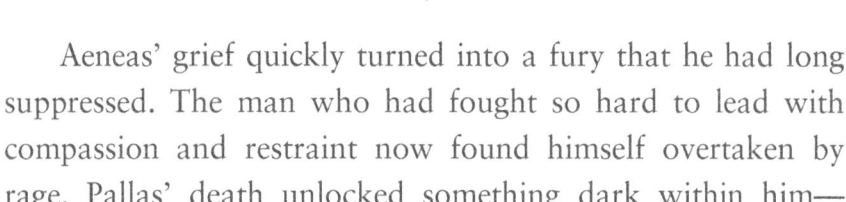

Aeneas' grief quickly turned into a fury that he had long suppressed. The man who had fought so hard to lead with compassion and restraint now found himself overtaken by rage. Pallas' death unlocked something dark within him—something primal. The love he had for the boy, the guilt of having failed to protect him, and the senselessness of his loss transformed Aeneas into a force of vengeance.

Leading the Trojans back into battle, Aeneas fought with an intensity that few had seen before. His sword struck with deadly precision, each blow a tribute to the memory of Pallas. His enemies fell before him, not just as combatants but as symbols of the pain he carried. Gone was the measured and restrained leader who sought peace even in war. In his place stood a man consumed by the desire to avenge the boy who had looked up to him with such trust.

Aeneas' wrath was terrifying, but it was also deeply human. It revealed a side of him that had always existed but had been tempered by his sense of duty and compassion. Now, those qualities seemed buried beneath the weight of his grief. Each swing of his sword seemed to echo the words he could not speak—the sorrow for Pallas, the anger at fate, the frustration of carrying a destiny that demanded more from him than any man should have to bear.

Even as Aeneas cut down his enemies, a part of him knew that this rage could not last. It was unsustainable, a fire that would burn him out if he let it. But in that moment, he did not care. All he could see was the face of Turnus—the man who had taken Pallas' life—and the need to end the war, whatever the cost.

# AENEAS 'LEGACY: ROME'S HISTORICAL FOUNDER THE FUTURE OF ROME

The war had been won, and peace had finally settled over the land, but for Aeneas, the journey was far from over. His story, etched in the hearts of his people, would live on, but it was his son, Ascanius, who would carry the torch forward. Ascanius, known to history as Iulus, took with him not only his father's name but the weight of the legacy Aeneas had fought so hard to establish.

In the quiet years after the war, Ascanius grew into a leader in his own right. Following his father's footsteps, he founded Alba Longa, a city that would become the cradle of Roman civilisation. Though Aeneas never lived to see it, his lineage continued through his son, and it was from this line that Rome's most legendary figures, Romulus and Remus, would eventually rise.

The prophecy that had been whispered to Aeneas in the World of the Ancestors, the future his father Anchises had shown him, was now coming to life. Aeneas had not simply fought to survive, nor had he led his people to safety just for their own sake—he had laid the foundation for an empire. The new city would grow and expand, and from it, Rome would emerge, the eternal city that would reshape the course of history.

# AENEAS' AS THE IDEAL ROMAN HERO

To understand Aeneas' legacy, one must look beyond the battles he fought or the cities he founded. Aeneas represented something far greater—he embodied the virtues that Rome itself would come to cherish. His story was not just one of conquest or victory, but one of duty, sacrifice, and unshakable resolve.

Throughout his journey, Aeneas demonstrated pietas—a devotion to the gods, to his family, and to the future of his people. He had every reason to surrender to despair. He had lost his home, his wife, and many of his closest companions. Yet, he never wavered in his commitment to the divine mandate placed upon him. Even when the gods asked him to leave behind the comforts of love with Queen Dido, he obeyed, knowing that his duty to the Trojans and to their destiny outweighed his personal happiness.

And there was his virtues—the courage and moral integrity that guided him, even in the darkest moments. When Aeneas raged after Pallas' death, he could have let anger consume him entirely, but he found his way back to the values that anchored him. Aeneas was not just a warrior, but a protector. His strength was tempered by compassion, his courage grounded in the knowledge that every decision he made would affect the future of countless generations.

In this, Aeneas became the prototype of the ideal Roman hero. He was not perfect, but he was unrelenting in his duty. He understood that his sacrifices—both personal and on the battlefield—were necessary to build something greater than himself. His willingness to endure the loss of Troy, the hardships of exile, and the pain of personal tragedies was not just about survival, but about creating the conditions for a legacy that would endure through the ages.

As future Roman leaders looked back upon their origins, they saw in Aeneas a mirror of the values they aspired to uphold. His life was a testament to the belief that true leadership required not just strength and courage, but a deep sense of responsibility to the greater good. It was this sense of duty, this unyielding devotion to the gods and to his people, that made Aeneas not just a hero of history, but the spiritual father of Rome itself.

# THE STORY OF BRUTUS: FROM EXILE TO KING OF BRITAIN BRUTUS 'EARLY YEARS AND EXILE

———◆———

The story of Brutus, the great-grandson of the heroic Aeneas, begins steeped in the ancient prophecies that had followed his Trojan bloodline through generations. Brutus was born in Rome, where the remnants of the Trojan people had tried to find peace after the fall of their city. As a descendant of Aeneas, Brutus was raised with the knowledge of his forefather's epic journey from the ruins of Troy and the heavy weight of the prophecy that foretold greatness—but also tragedy—for those who bore his name.

From a young age, Brutus was shaped by this legacy, understanding that his blood tied him to a great destiny. His father, Silvius, spoke often of the future, of the old stories told by Aeneas himself. There were whispers that a child of the Trojan line would rise to found a new empire, a new Troy, but this future was shrouded in sorrow. It was said that this child would also bring untold suffering upon his own kin.

As Brutus grew older, this prophecy began to hang over him like a storm cloud. Though only a boy, he felt the burden of fate in every word spoken about his lineage. His mother, Aeneas' granddaughter, passed away when Brutus was still very young, leaving him with only his father to guide him. His father's teachings were a mix of pride and caution, for he too feared the destiny written in the stars for his son.

# THE FATAL ACCIDENT AND EXILE

The tragic day that would forever change Brutus' life came without warning. During a royal hunt in the Roman forests, Brutus, still barely more than a boy, accidentally loosed an arrow that found its mark in his own father, Silvius. The once-prophetic words of doom now felt like a cruel twist of fate, fulfilled by the hand of the very child they had warned about.

But fate, ever capricious, intervened. As Brutus drew back the bowstring, a sudden shift in the wind, unpredictable and cruel, caused his aim to falter. The arrow, released with all his youthful fervour, deviated from its intended path. In a heartbeat, it found its tragic mark—not in the stag, but in the heart of his beloved father.

The forest fell silent. Silvius staggered, a look of disbelief mingled with sorrow etched upon his features. Brutus, frozen in horror, could only watch as his father crumpled to the ground. The realisation of what had happened crashed over him like a tidal wave of grief and guilt. The lesson of the bow—the sacred trust—had been shattered in an instant.

In the agonising moments that followed, Silvius, his breaths shallow and his life slipping away, managed to grasp Brutus' hand. With his fading strength, he whispered words of love and forgiveness, urging his son to remember that even in the darkest misfortune, there lay a lesson to guide the future. "Forgive me, my son," he murmured, his voice barely audible. "May you find the strength to transform this tragedy into a legacy of hope. Let our blood be a beacon, not a curse."

Brutus was devastated. The weight of his mistake, coupled with the ever-present prophecy, now seemed unbearable. His father's death at his own hand was seen not only as a personal tragedy but as an omen. Rome began to murmur that the young Brutus was cursed, and some believed he had been destined to bring misfortune upon his family and people.

With his father gone, Brutus became an outcast, unable to escape the shadow of guilt that haunted him. His relatives, unwilling to defy the old prophecy, decided that for the good of Rome, he must leave. They could no longer risk the presence of a boy destined for both greatness and ruin. He was exiled, sent away to roam foreign lands and to carry the weight of his family's fall with him.

# A NEW LIFE IN GREECE

Brutus fled Rome, his heart heavy with sorrow and confusion. He sailed across the sea and eventually found himself in Greece, a land that had long been hostile to the Trojans. Greece was still a place where the memories of the Trojan War were fresh in the minds of its people, and Brutus, though disguised as an exile, bore the bloodline of the city they had once destroyed.

Despite the enmity that lingered, Greece became a place where Brutus could rebuild himself. Here, among the ruins of his past and the ashes of his people's former enemies, he found a new path. The Greeks had taken in many of the surviving Trojans as slaves, forcing them into a life of servitude. Yet, Brutus was no ordinary Trojan, and in his veins burned the legacy of a great hero.

Under the guidance of skilled Greek officers, Brutus was trained in the arts of war. He grew into a formidable warrior and leader, mastering the tactics and strategies that would later become essential in his rise to power. As he fought alongside the Greeks, his Trojan heritage, once a curse, began to inspire those who suffered under Greek rule.

# THE STIRRING OF REBELLION

Brutus' arrival in Greece marked the beginning of a new chapter, but it was one filled with shadows. For generations, the Trojans had languished in bondage under their Greek captors, remnants of a once-great civilisation now scattered and enslaved. They laboured under the weight of their ancestors' defeat, their pride buried beneath years of servitude. Their memories of Troy had faded into stories told in hushed tones, and their dreams of freedom seemed like distant echoes of a forgotten time.

But Brutus was different. He wasn't just another Trojan slave. He bore the bloodline of Aeneas, the legendary hero who had survived the fall of Troy, and with it, the hope of an entire people. Though young, Brutus carried the weight of destiny on his shoulders, and the enslaved Trojans saw in him a spark of something they thought they had lost forever: the possibility of freedom.

The whispers of rebellion began long before swords were sharpened. At first, it was just murmurs in the dark, in the kitchens where slaves toiled or the barracks where they slept—rumours of a Trojan descendant who had come to Greece. The old men and women who had once told their children of Troy's fall began to speak of Brutus, the last hope of their people. For the younger generations, who had never known freedom, this idea seemed both impossible and intoxicating.

# BRUTUS'
# TRANSFORMATION
# INTO A LEADER

At first, Brutus didn't see himself as a leader. He had come to Greece to escape his guilt, to flee the shadow of his father's death, not to lead a rebellion. But as he grew into manhood, trained by the Greeks in the ways of war, he could not ignore the plight of his people. He saw the strength in their eyes, the fire that had not yet been extinguished by years of servitude. Slowly, the idea of rebellion began to take root in his heart, planted by the very people who believed in him.

The more Brutus saw of the Greeks, the more he understood their weaknesses. They had grown complacent, arrogant in their dominance over the Trojans, believing that the spirit of Troy had died along with its walls. But Brutus knew better. He began to organise the Trojans in secret, gathering them under the pretence of labor or under the cover of night. What started as small, clandestine meetings quickly grew into something more. Brutus' natural charisma drew them in—men and women, young and old. He listened to their stories, their grievances, and slowly, he began to unite them.

In the hidden corners of Greece, far from the eyes of their Greek masters, the Trojans began to forge weapons from whatever they could find. Old farm tools became spears; stolen iron became blades. Brutus' training in warfare became invaluable as he taught the Trojans how to fight, how to defend themselves, and how to strike when the time was right.

The night was still, the air heavy with the whispers of men who had long learned to speak in hushed tones, lest their voices be carried to the ears of their captors. Brutus sat alone in the dim glow of an oil lamp, his quill poised above parchment, his mind a battlefield of unspoken words. His people, the last of the Trojan exiles, had endured generations of servitude under the Greeks. They had been allowed to live, to work, to bear children—but always under the yoke of another's rule. They had not forgotten their origins, but in time, they had learned to survive by suppressing them.

# BRUTUS COULD NOT ACCEPT THIS.

His blood carried the fire of Aeneas, the memory of fallen Troy, the whispers of a divine promise that had yet to be fulfilled. The time for silence had ended. With measured breaths, he pressed his quill to the parchment and began to write—to address King Pandrasus, the ruler of the Greeks, the man who held his people in an invisible prison.

If freedom was to come, it would first be demanded.

With every stroke of ink, Brutus crafted words that were not merely requests but indictments. He did not beg for mercy or plead for goodwill; he laid forth a truth that could not be ignored.

# "GREAT KING PANDRASUS,

For too long, we, the sons of Troy, have laboured under your dominion. Once, we were warriors and kings, but now we have become luxurious slaves—allowed to wear fine garments but denied the honor of sovereignty, fed with the spoils of toil but never allowed to claim them as our own. Is this the fate of a people whose ancestors defied the might of Greece for ten long years? Is this the destiny of those who once stood at the gates of Olympus itself?"

His hands tightened around the quill as he continued, his pulse steady, his resolve unwavering.

"You allow us to live, but you deny us our right to be free men. You grant us land to till, but you claim the harvest for your own. You call us allies, yet we must bow before your every decree. If it is your wish to rule over willing subjects, then you must recognise that we, the people of Troy, are not among them. We are not Greek. We never were, and we never shall be. The blood of Aeneas does not kneel—it rises.

We do not seek war. We seek only what is just: that we be permitted to leave in peace and take our destiny into our own hands. Let us part as men of reason, not as adversaries. Release us from these gilded chains, and we shall take our leave of your lands, never again to trouble your rule.

Deny us, and you will learn that even in chains, the spirit of Troy is unbroken."

Brutus sealed the letter with the emblem of his house—the lion of Troy, the silent echo of a city that had fallen but had not been forgotten. He knew what he had written would enrage Pandrasus, but the Greek king needed to see the truth in unrelenting clarity. His words were not empty rhetoric; they were the foundation of a movement that had already begun.

# PANDRASUS' REACTION: THE SPARK OF WAR

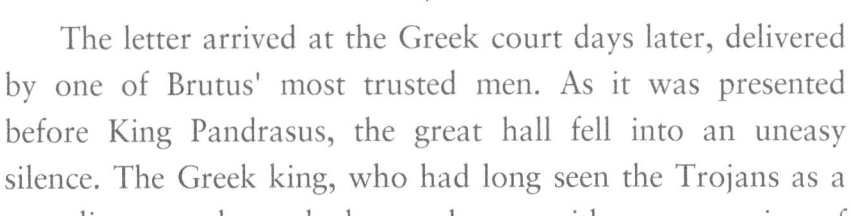

The letter arrived at the Greek court days later, delivered by one of Brutus' most trusted men. As it was presented before King Pandrasus, the great hall fell into an uneasy silence. The Greek king, who had long seen the Trojans as a compliant people, took the parchment with an expression of indifference—until his eyes scanned the first few lines.

With each word he read, his expression darkened. His jaw tightened. His grip on the parchment turned his knuckles white. The audacity! The arrogance! He stood abruptly, the force of his movement causing the letter to crumple slightly in his grasp. His advisors, sensing his fury, exchanged uneasy glances. No one dared to speak.

"Luxurious slaves?" Pandrasus repeated aloud, his voice laced with venom. "He dares to say this to me? That I have fed them, clothed them, given them refuge, only to be repaid with treachery?"

He paced the chamber, his rage mounting. He had tolerated the Trojans, allowed them their customs, even treated them as something resembling equals. And yet, here was Brutus, speaking as though his people had been shackled like common criminals. His pride could not accept this insult.

"This is a call to rebellion," he spat, turning to his commanders. "Brutus does not seek freedom. He seeks to defy me—to challenge my authority in my own land. If he desires war, then war he shall have. Send word to my generals. We march at once."

With that decree, the fate of both men was sealed.

Brutus had known Pandrasus would not accept his demand without resistance. The Greek king's pride would never allow it. But war had already been set in motion—not by swords, but by words that struck harder than any weapon.

The Trojans, hearing of Pandrasus' fury, did not shrink in fear. They rose.


Brutus' letter had not only angered a king—it had awakened a people. The Trojan blood that had remained dormant for too long now burned with new purpose. No longer would they be content with survival alone. They were ready to fight for the freedom they had been denied.

As the Greek forces prepared for war, Brutus stood before his people, the firelight of their encampment casting flickering shadows on his face. He held no illusions—this would be a war hard-fought. But his voice was steady, his conviction unshaken.

"We were once Trojans," he said, his voice carrying over the gathered warriors. "And we shall be Trojans once more. No more will we bow. No more will we serve. Tonight, we reclaim our destiny."

And with that, the rebellion began.

# THE FIRE OF REBELLION IGNITES

For months, the rebellion simmered beneath the surface. Brutus knew that patience was key. The Greeks, though powerful, were scattered across the land, and a single ill-timed rebellion could be easily crushed. Brutus was careful, calculating each step. He understood that the success of this uprising depended not on force alone, but on strategy. He needed to strike when the Greeks were at their weakest.

Finally, the moment came. A Greek festival—a time when their oppressors would be distracted, drunk on wine and victory, their guard lowered. Brutus knew it was the perfect opportunity to ignite the fire that had been smouldering for so long.

The night of the rebellion began quietly. Trojan slaves moved through the Greek camps with purpose, slipping into the shadows, gathering in the designated meeting spots that Brutus had chosen. The signal came with the sound of a single horn—long and low, carried on the wind. It was the sound of liberation, the sound of Troy rising once more.

# THE BATTLE FOR FREEDOM

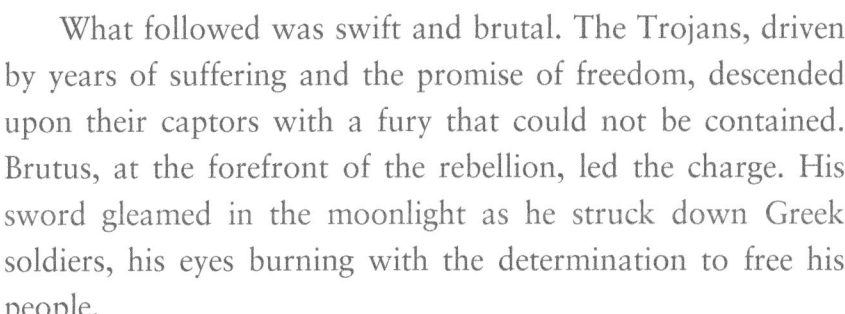

What followed was swift and brutal. The Trojans, driven by years of suffering and the promise of freedom, descended upon their captors with a fury that could not be contained. Brutus, at the forefront of the rebellion, led the charge. His sword gleamed in the moonlight as he struck down Greek soldiers, his eyes burning with the determination to free his people.

The Greeks, caught off guard, scrambled to defend themselves. But Brutus had planned well. The Greeks' forces were scattered, uncoordinated, and unable to mount a proper defence against the sudden uprising. Trojan warriors, once slaves, fought with the strength of men who had nothing left to lose. They fought for their lives, their families, and the dream of a new future.

Brutus himself became a beacon on the battlefield, his presence igniting hope in his people and fear in the hearts of the Greeks. He fought not just with skill, but with a righteous fury that had been building within him for years. He fought for the father he had lost, for the mother he barely remembered, and for the people who had suffered under the yoke of oppression for far too long.

# THE TRIUMPH OF THE TROJANS

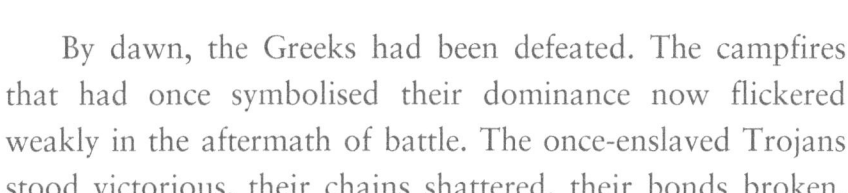

By dawn, the Greeks had been defeated. The campfires that had once symbolised their dominance now flickered weakly in the aftermath of battle. The once-enslaved Trojans stood victorious, their chains shattered, their bonds broken. The rebellion had succeeded, and Brutus had led them to freedom.

In the moments after the battle, Brutus stood among his people, the weight of what they had achieved settling upon him. He had led the Trojans to victory, but the road ahead was still uncertain. They were free, but they were also without a home. Greece had been a prison, but it had also been their refuge. Now, they were truly exiles, cast out into the world once more.

But as the sun rose over the blood-soaked fields, Brutus felt a renewed sense of purpose. The rebellion was only the beginning. The prophecy that had followed him since birth whispered in his ear, reminding him that his journey was far from over. He had freed his people from slavery, but now he would lead them to a new home—a place where they could rebuild, where the spirit of Troy would rise again.

The Trojans looked to Brutus not just as their saviour, but as their leader, their king. The fire of rebellion had ignited something far greater than freedom—it had sparked the beginning of a new chapter in the history of their people. And Brutus, with the blood of Aeneas running through his veins, would lead them to that future.

# THE VISION OF DIANA AND THE SEARCH FOR A NEW TROY

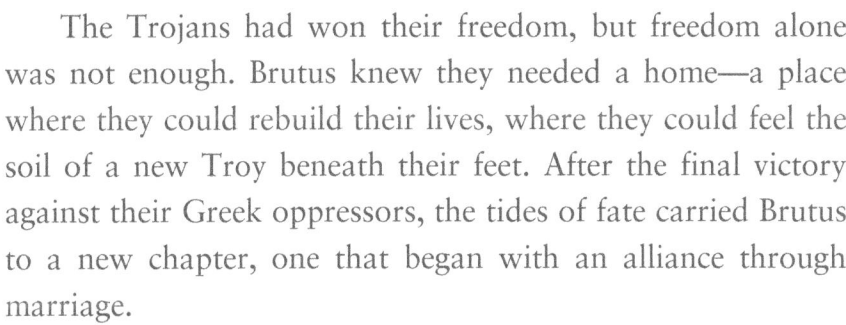

The Trojans had won their freedom, but freedom alone was not enough. Brutus knew they needed a home—a place where they could rebuild their lives, where they could feel the soil of a new Troy beneath their feet. After the final victory against their Greek oppressors, the tides of fate carried Brutus to a new chapter, one that began with an alliance through marriage.

# A UNION WITH THE KING'S DAUGHTER

As a gesture of goodwill and alliance, the Greek King Pandrasus offered his daughter, Ignoge, in marriage to Brutus. This was more than a mere diplomatic gesture; it

was a recognition of Brutus' strength and the respect he had earned even from his former adversaries. Ignoge, the daughter of Pandrasus, was a woman of both grace and intelligence, and her presence brought a sense of stability and partnership that Brutus had never known.

Their marriage was celebrated with grandeur, a rare moment of joy and peace amidst the turmoil of their lives. Ignoge stood beside Brutus, offering him not only her hand but also a reminder of the life they sought to build together. With Ignoge at his side, Brutus felt his resolve strengthen. She was his partner now, and together they would forge a path for their people.

King Pandrasus, respecting Brutus as an honourable leader and now family, bestowed upon him a fleet of ships to carry the Trojans wherever their destiny called. With these vessels, Brutus and his people could finally set out to fulfil the prophecy that had shadowed him since birth. But before he could set sail, Brutus needed guidance. He needed to know the path the gods had chosen for him, and for that, he would seek out the goddess Diana.

# THE SACRED RITUAL ON DIANA'S ISLAND

Guided by ancient lore and the wisdom of his priests, Brutus sailed with his people to a remote island known for its sacred temple to Diana, goddess of the hunt, the moon, and new beginnings. This island, shrouded in mist and ancient woods, was a place of quiet reverence, where the boundary between the mortal and divine seemed almost transparent.

Upon arriving, Brutus and his priests made their way to the ancient temple nestled within a grove of towering oak trees. The air was thick with the scent of wild herbs, and the distant sound of waves crashing against the shore underscored the solemnity of the moment. The temple itself was simple but imbued with an aura of mysticism—its stone walls overgrown with vines, and its altar bearing the marks of countless rituals that had come before.

In the stillness of the night, under the watchful gaze of the moon, Brutus prepared for the sacred rite. His priests gathered around the altar, chanting hymns to invoke the goddess, their voices weaving through the trees like a whispered prayer. Brutus stood at the centre, holding a sacrificial offering—a white stag, symbolising purity and the unspoiled land they sought. He knew that if Diana was to bless their journey, he needed to approach her with humility and reverence.

Brutus knelt before the altar, lifting his hands to the heavens, and spoke with a voice that carried both hope and desperation. "Diana, goddess of the wild and the protector of those who wander, I come to you in search of guidance. We are a people adrift, freed from our chains but still without a home. Show us the land where we can rebuild, where the spirit of Troy can rise once more."

# DIANA'S PROPHECY

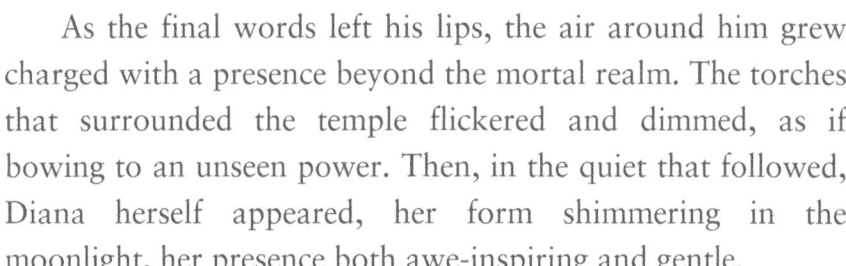

As the final words left his lips, the air around him grew charged with a presence beyond the mortal realm. The torches that surrounded the temple flickered and dimmed, as if bowing to an unseen power. Then, in the quiet that followed, Diana herself appeared, her form shimmering in the moonlight, her presence both awe-inspiring and gentle.

"Brutus, son of Troy," Diana spoke, her voice like the rustling leaves, each word a melody that filled the grove with a serene energy. "You have fought bravely and freed your people, but your journey is not yet complete. I will show you the path to your new home—a land of promise, where your descendants will flourish."

Brutus listened intently, his heart pounding with anticipation.

"You will cross the vast waters," Diana continued, her eyes alight with an otherworldly wisdom, "until you find an island. It will be a land of giants, a land where the white deer roam free. This land shall be yours, where you will build a new Troy, a city greater than the one your ancestors lost. There, you shall reign, and your line will give rise to a people destined to shape the world."

Brutus held his breath, the weight of her words settling over him like a cloak of both honour and responsibility. He knew that Diana was guiding him to a place far beyond anything he had dreamed.

"But beware, Brutus," Diana warned, her tone shifting to one of caution, "for the path to your new Troy will not be easy. You will face trials that will test the very fabric of your spirit. You must hold steadfast, for only through strength and unity will you claim this land. This is your destiny, and the future of your people depends upon it."

With those final words, Diana's form began to fade, her image dissolving into the moonlit mist as swiftly as it had appeared. The grove fell silent once more, but Brutus could still feel the pulse of her presence, the certainty that the goddess had bestowed upon him a divine mission.

# THE PATH FORWARD

Brutus rose from his knees, his mind a flurry of thoughts, his heart filled with a new sense of purpose. Diana had spoken directly to him, had entrusted him with the fate of his people, and he knew that he could not fail them. Returning to his priests and his people, he recounted Diana's prophecy, her exact words etched into his memory like a map to their future.

With the fleet granted by King Pandrasus, Brutus and the Trojans set sail from the island with renewed determination. They were not simply wanderers anymore; they were a people chosen by the gods, destined for greatness in a land yet unseen. Ignoge stood beside him on the deck of the lead ship, her hand resting in his, her eyes filled with a mixture of wonder and resolve.

The voyage ahead would be long and fraught with peril, but Brutus had the blessing of Diana and the courage of his ancestors guiding him. He would cross the waters, seek the land of giants, and build a new Troy—a land where his people could finally find peace, and where the legacy of Troy would live on, reborn and undaunted.

# THE JOURNEY OF BRUTUS
# AND KERNOW TO
# AMORICA AND BEYOND

With Diana's prophecy etched deeply into his heart, Brutus set sail with his people, his new bride Ignoge, and a small fleet granted to him by King Pandrasus. Their journey across the seas was filled with a mixture of hope and trepidation. They knew not where their new home lay, but they knew it awaited them somewhere beyond the horizon. Brutus was a man driven by destiny, but he also knew that he could not achieve it alone. It was during this uncertain time, as they approached the southern coast of France, that Brutus encountered the man who would become his most steadfast ally—Kernow.

The Trojans landed near the mouth of the Rhône River, where they were greeted not by peace, but by the harsh reality of the land. The region was ruled by warlike tribes, and Brutus knew that finding allies here would not be easy. Yet, as he scouted the area, he encountered a group of travellers—exiles like his own people—who were camped near the rugged coastline. Among them was a man of extraordinary size and strength, a warrior with a commanding presence and a gleam of mischief in his eye. His name was Kernow.

Kernow was a giant of a man, known far and wide for his feats of strength and bravery. Originally from a land even farther north, Kernow had come to southern France in search of new battles, eager to prove his might against worthy foes. His reputation had preceded him, and Brutus had heard tales of a warrior who could wrestle beasts with his bare hands. Intrigued by the stories, Brutus sought him out, and the two men quickly discovered a kinship between them. Both were exiles, warriors, and leaders bound by the fate of their people.

Brutus saw in Kernow not only a formidable ally but a brother-in-arms. Kernow, for his part, was drawn to Brutus' sense of purpose and his vision for a new homeland. The two men shared stories of their travels, their losses, and their dreams. They spoke of the ancient prophecies that had led them to this place, and Brutus told Kernow of Diana's vision—the land of the giants, where he would build a new Troy.

"Why not here?" Kernow asked, gesturing to the rich land around them. "The people here are fierce, but so are we. We could carve out a home among them."

Brutus, however, shook his head. "This is not the place Diana spoke of. Her words were clear—we must find an island where the white deer roam free, a land that will welcome us and challenge us in equal measure. Still, let us journey together, for there is strength in unity, and the path to our destiny may yet take us through Amorica."

And so, with a bond forged in shared purpose, Brutus and Kernow set out together, leading their people into the heart of Amorica—what would later be known as Brittany.

# BATTLING THE CHIEFS
# OF AMORICA

The lands of Amorica were wild and untamed, ruled by local chieftains who were quick to defend their territories. The people were hardy and suspicious of outsiders, and Brutus knew that to win their respect, he would need to prove his strength. Together with Kernow, he led his people through the dense forests and rocky hills, seeking out the chieftains who ruled these lands.

The battles were fierce and relentless. The chiefs of Amorica did not yield easily, and their warriors met the Trojans with a ferocity that matched their own. Brutus, alongside Kernow, fought with a skill honed through years of hardship and training. Kernow, wielding his enormous club, became a force of nature on the battlefield, his laughter booming as he swept through ranks of enemies, scattering them like leaves in a storm.

Though their opponents were strong, the Trojans were driven by a purpose that transcended the struggle for land. They fought not just to survive, but to fulfil a prophecy, and in each battle, Brutus felt Diana's words echoing within him, reminding him that this was not their final destination.

One by one, the Amorican chieftains fell, and Brutus and Kernow secured a tenuous peace. The locals, seeing the might and resolve of the Trojans, began to acknowledge their strength. They offered temporary shelter and provisions, but Brutus could not ignore the feeling that something was amiss. Even as they settled, he felt a restlessness within him, a gnawing sense that Amorica was not the promised land.

# REALISING AMORICA WAS NOT THE LAND OF PROPHECY

In the quiet moments after the battles had subsided, Brutus reflected on Diana's words. He had expected the signs of destiny to reveal themselves here, but the land felt too familiar, too earthly, to be the one of which she spoke. The visions of a white deer and an untamed island haunted his dreams, and he knew, deep in his heart, that Amorica was merely a waypoint, not the end of their journey.

He shared his thoughts with Kernow, who had grown fond of the land and the challenges it had provided. "This is a strong place," Kernow said, "and we could build something here. But if Diana's words do not match this land, then perhaps we are yet to find what we seek."

Brutus nodded, the weight of destiny pressing upon him once more. "We are still bound for the island that Diana described. This land is rich, and the people are strong, but it is not the land of giants. It is not the place where our true destiny lies."

With a heavy heart but a renewed resolve, Brutus made the difficult decision to leave Amorica. He gathered the Trojans and explained the vision once more, sharing with them the conviction that they must press onward. Some were reluctant, having grown attached to the land they had fought to conquer, but they trusted Brutus, and his words rekindled their faith.

Kernow, ever loyal, stood by his side. "If there is yet a land of giants to conquer, then I shall go with you. Together we will find this place, and together we will make it our own."

# JOURNEY TO THE ISLAND OF BRITAIN

And so, Brutus and Kernow led their people back to their ships, setting their sights on the vast sea that lay before them. As the Trojans left the shores of Amorica, they felt the pull of the unknown, the promise of an island where their destiny awaited. The seas were rough, and the journey was fraught with uncertainty, but they pressed on, driven by the vision Diana had bestowed upon Brutus.

After days upon the waves, the Trojans spotted land—a mist-covered island emerging on the horizon, wild and untamed. As they approached, Brutus felt a surge of excitement and fear. This, he knew, was the land Diana had spoken of, a place both foreign and familiar, a land where his people could finally lay down roots and build a new Troy.

When they reached the shores, the Trojans disembarked with reverence, their feet touching the soil of what would become their new home. The island was inhabited by a strange and ancient people, and Brutus knew that this was only the beginning of a new adventure. But with Kernow by his side and the prophecy guiding his steps, Brutus felt ready to embrace the destiny that awaited them.

Together, Brutus and Kernow would carve out a place for their people on this island, a land that would come to be known as Britain. Here, they would build a new city, a new Troy, and a new beginning. The journey had been long and the trials many, but Brutus felt that he had finally found the land of his destiny.

# THE PROPHECY OF THE ABORIGINES AND THE CORONATION OF BRUTUS

As Brutus and his followers traveled deeper into the island of Britain, they encountered a people whose presence and history reached back through countless generations. These were the Aborigines of Britain, descendants of a diaspora from lands once known as Lemuria and Mu, ancient and sophisticated civilisations from regions we now associate with Sri Lanka, Indonesia, and the Andaman Sea. This was a people who held knowledge of lands submerged by time, lands linked to the Ancient Kingdom of the Kongo, which connected distant continents through a web of ancient trade and cultural exchange.

The Aborigines had preserved the memory of their origins and the stories of their ancestors. They lived in harmony with the land, knowledgeable in its secrets and guardians of its sacred sites. As Brutus and his people arrived, they found themselves welcomed with a curiosity that belied a deeper understanding. The Aborigines recognised Brutus as more than a wandering leader; they saw in him the fulfilment of a prophecy handed down through generations.

According to the Aborigines, there existed an ancient prophecy that foretold the arrival of a foreign leader descended from a "great and ancient city" beyond the seas. This leader, the prophecy claimed, would be of noble lineage, carrying the legacy of a civilisation that had once flourished and then fallen. He would bring with him a people searching for a new beginning, and he would become their king, guiding them to prosperity and peace.

When Brutus and his followers shared their story—the fall of Troy, the prophecy of Diana, and their search for a new home—the Aborigines felt the stirrings of recognition. Here was a leader from the storied city of Troy, a descendant of heroes who had weathered centuries of upheaval and had come to their island with a vision of rebirth. To the Aborigines, Brutus was the one foretold in their ancient prophecy, a man destined to lead and protect their land.

# AVEBURY: THE STONE CIRCLE OF DOMINIUM

The Aborigines led Brutus and his people to Avebury, a stone circle revered as a place of wisdom and power. This ancient site, known as the Circle of Dominium, had been a gathering place for generations, a site where leaders were anointed and decisions of great consequence were made. The stones, weathered by time, stood as silent witnesses to centuries of history, their presence a reminder of the enduring legacy of those who had come before.

It was within this circle that Brutus' coronation was to take place. The Aborigines, with Brutus' people standing alongside them, gathered around the stones, their faces illuminated by the warm glow of firelight. The air was thick with reverence as Brutus stepped forward to accept his new role. He knelt in the centre of the circle, surrounded by the towering stones, a man who had traveled from a faraway land to fulfil a destiny that had been waiting for him long before he was born.

One of the elders of the Aborigines, a respected leader whose lineage traced back to the days of Lemuria, stepped forward to preside over the ceremony. With solemnity, he recited the ancient words of the prophecy, invoking the spirits of the ancestors who had once walked these lands and guided their people. He spoke of the unity between Brutus and the island, a bond that would bring harmony and prosperity to both the newcomers and the Aborigines.

The Coronation of Brutus

As the elder completed his invocation, he placed a crown of woven branches upon Brutus' head, symbolising his role as a leader in harmony with the land. In that moment, Brutus became the first king of Britain, recognised not only by his own people but by the Aborigines as well. It was a moment of profound unity, a blending of cultures and histories that reached across time and space.

Brutus rose to his feet, looking out at the faces of those gathered around him—his people, the Aborigines, and the elders who held the wisdom of ages. He felt the weight of his new title, not as a burden, but as an honour, an opportunity to fulfil his promise to build a new home where peace and prosperity could thrive.

The people hailed him as the founder of a new Troy, and as their voices rose in unison, Brutus felt the deep connection

that now bound him to the land and to the people who had accepted him as their king. In that ancient circle, beneath the gaze of the stones, he became not just a leader, but a symbol of a future forged from the wisdom of the past and the promise of unity.

With this coronation, Brutus had fulfilled the prophecy of the Aborigines and laid the foundation for a new era. The island was now theirs, a place where they could rebuild, where Trojan heritage would blend with ancient traditions from Lemuria and the lands of the Kongo. The legacy of Troy, intertwined with the ancient wisdom of the Aborigines, would shape the destiny of Britain for generations to come.

Brutus' Reign and the Founding of New Troy

After his coronation, Brutus began the immense task of establishing his kingdom in the land that would come to be known as Britain. Guided by the dreams of his ancestors and the prophecy of Diana, he chose a strategic location in the west to build his city—a place where the River Thames met the fertile land, with easy access to the sea and a vantage point over the surrounding territories. This land held promise, and it would become the cradle of his vision: Troia Nova, or New Troy.

# THE FOUNDING OF TROIA NOVA

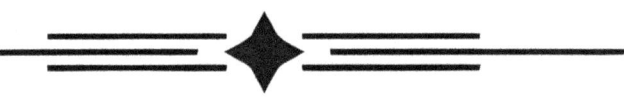

The construction of Troia Nova was a labor of love, one that involved both the newly arrived Trojans and the native Aborigines. Brutus' leadership and vision for the city inspired both groups to work side by side. They raised walls from the earth, constructed homes and temples, and established marketplaces and halls where the people could gather. The foundation stones of Troia Nova were laid with care and reverence, each block a symbol of hope for a new beginning.

Brutus took an active role in the city's construction, often seen among his people as they worked. He was not a king who sat idle in a throne room—he shared in their labor, his hands as rough and calloused as those of the builders, his voice a constant encouragement. To the people, he was not only their king but a part of their lives, a figure they could look for both guidance and camaraderie.

In tribute to the fallen city of his ancestors, Brutus made sure that the heart of Troia Nova echoed the spirit of old Troy. He commissioned statues of the Trojan heroes and established rituals that honoured their memory. Yet, he also encouraged his people to forge new traditions, ones that reflected their journey and the land they now called home. This blend of past and present created a unique culture within Troia Nova, a culture that celebrated resilience and unity.

# A KINGDOM OF PROSPERITY AND PEACE

As the years passed, Troia Nova flourished under Brutus' rule. He proved himself a wise and just king, one who understood that strength lay not only in arms but in the hearts and minds of his people. Brutus established councils where both Trojans and Aborigines could speak freely, ensuring that all voices were heard. He valued wisdom and fairness, making decisions that balanced justice with compassion.

Brutus' reign saw the development of agriculture and trade, which brought prosperity to the kingdom. The fields surrounding Troia Nova yielded bountiful harvests, and the rivers teemed with fish. Brutus encouraged his people to engage in trade with neighbouring tribes, strengthening alliances and building relationships that would safeguard the future of his kingdom. Craftsmen and artisans flourished, their skills adding beauty and functionality to the city, and Troia Nova began to gain a reputation as a place of both innovation and tradition.

Under Brutus' guidance, the Trojans and Aborigines shared their knowledge and skills, blending their cultural practices into a harmonious whole. Together, they celebrated festivals and honoured the cycles of nature, forging a bond that transcended their origins. In this way, Brutus not only founded a city but also laid the groundwork for a diverse and inclusive society, one that would become the bedrock of a new civilisation.

# THE SPIRIT OF TROY REBORN

For twenty-four years, Brutus ruled over Troia Nova, shaping it into a city that embodied the spirit of resilience. He often reflected on the journey that had brought them here—from the ashes of Troy, through battles and exile, to the land that Diana had promised. Brutus knew that the memory of old Troy could have been a source of sorrow, a reminder of what they had lost. But he chose instead to make it a beacon of strength, a testament to the endurance of his people.

The Trojans found solace in Brutus' leadership and pride in their new city. They taught their children the stories of old Troy, not as a tragedy, but as a tale of survival and rebirth. They sang songs of the heroes who had fought to protect their homeland, and they honoured Brutus as a king who had fulfilled their destiny by creating a new Troy in the heart of Britain.

Brutus' reign was marked by a deep connection to his people. He often walked among them, listening to their concerns and sharing in their joys. He attended births, weddings, and harvest celebrations, his presence a reminder that he was not above his people, but one of them. This kinship fostered a sense of unity that became the core of Troia Nova's strength.

In time, the name Troia Nova would evolve into London, but the spirit of its founder would remain. Brutus' legacy endured not just in the physical structures he built, but in the resilience he inspired in his people. The city grew, adapting to the changes that came with each new generation, yet the memory of Brutus' vision continued to guide it. He had given them more than a home; he had given them a purpose, a reason to believe that no matter how far they traveled or how much they lost, they could always rebuild and thrive.

# BRUTUS 'ENDURING LEGACY

As Brutus neared the end of his life, he looked upon Troia Nova with a heart full of pride. He had fulfilled his destiny, leading his people to a land where they could not only survive but flourish. He knew that he had laid the foundations of a kingdom that would endure beyond his lifetime, a city that would one day become a symbol of power and civilisation.

In his final days, Brutus shared his wisdom with those who would follow him, ensuring that the values of justice, unity, and resilience would be passed down through the generations. When he finally passed, he was mourned by all who knew him—Trojans and Aborigines alike. They laid him to rest within the city he had built, honouring him as both a king and a father.

Brutus' story is the original story of the indigenous people of Britain, but his legacy remained tangible in the stones of Troia Nova and in the hearts of its people. He had transformed the memory of Troy from one of ruin into a legacy of hope. Under his reign, New Troy had risen from the ashes, a city born of resilience and destined to shape the world. The journey of Brutus had begun with loss, but it had ended with the founding of an enduring empire, a testament to the strength and spirit of a people who refused to be forgotten.

Brutus of Troy, a historical figure in British history, is often referred to as both a Priest-King or Warrior-Priest due to his symbolic role as a ruler who embodied both spiritual leadership and military prowess. His portrayal as a founding figure of Britain in Geoffrey of Monmouth's Historia Regum Britanniae (History of the Kings of Britain) combines elements of both sacred and martial authority, making him a hybrid figure who straddled the divine and the earthly realms.

## 1. Priest-King: Spiritual Leadership

**Sacred Ancestry:** Brutus was believed to be a descendant of Aeneas, the Trojan hero, who in turn was a son of Venus, the Roman goddess of love. This divine ancestry contributed to the notion of Brutus as a figure with divine sanction. His lineage placed him in a position of spiritual authority, with a mandate to not only govern but also to act as a conduit of divine will.

**Founding a Sacred Kingdom:** As the historical founder of Britain, Brutus is portrayed as more than a military conqueror. His role as a Priest-King can be seen in his responsibility for establishing a new land where the people could live in accordance with the gods' will. He wasn't just carving out territory through conquest but also founding a new, sacred society, one that would be governed by laws believed to be rooted in divine justice (the so-called "Codes of Brutus").

**Lawgiver Role:** Brutus is credited with laying down the early laws for Britain, and his laws were often seen as divinely inspired, a key characteristic of a Priest-King. These laws would form the foundation of society's moral and civic life, blending religious duty with governance.

## 2. Warrior-Priest: Martial Leadership with a Sacred Duty.

**Military Leadership:** Brutus led the Trojan survivors after the fall of Troy on a long and perilous journey to find a new homeland. His ability to lead and protect his people through warfare and conquest was essential to his role as a Warrior. He conquered the giants and enemies he found in Britain, symbolising his role as a protector of his people and their newly found land.

**Sacred Combat:** In ancient traditions, particularly in Indo-European cultures, warriors were often seen as having sacred responsibilities. Combat wasn't just about territorial gain; it was viewed as fulfilling divine purposes. Brutus's battles to conquer Britain could be interpreted as sacred warfare—the fulfilment of his destiny to found a kingdom under the guidance of the gods. The Druids and other priestly figures in

Celtic societies saw war as a sacred act when performed in defence of the tribe, its lands, or divine order.

**Balance of Sacred and Martial Roles:** As a Warrior-Priest, Brutus represents the ideal leader in ancient histories: one who could defend the people through strength and valour in battle, while also acting as a mediator between the human and divine realms, ensuring that laws, governance, and society aligned with sacred principles.

## 3. Priest-King in the Celtic and Druidic Tradition

**Celtic Influence:** The concept of the Priest-King or Warrior-Priest in British history may be influenced by Celtic traditions, where kingship was closely linked with the spiritual realm. In early Celtic societies, kings were often seen as having a divine mandate to rule. They were responsible for maintaining the harmony between the people, the land, and the gods.

**Druids and Kingship:** The Druids, as the spiritual leaders of Celtic society, played an essential role in advising kings and ensuring that their reign was in accordance with divine will. A king who acted with both spiritual insight and military strength was seen as the ideal ruler, ensuring both the physical and spiritual well-being of the people.

**Sacred Kingship:** Celtic kings were often viewed as having sacred marriages to the land, with their role as king being spiritually sanctioned. Brutus, in this sense, could be seen as an early embodiment of this sacred kingship tradition, where his leadership combined both military prowess and spiritual stewardship.

## 4. Priest-King and Warrior-Priest in Classical and Indo-European Tradition

**Classical Precedents:** Brutus's dual role as Priest-King or Warrior-Priest echoes other Indo-European traditions, where rulers often held both religious and military authority. In ancient Greece and Rome, rulers were often responsible for leading religious ceremonies as well as commanding armies, a tradition that could have influenced the depiction of Brutus in British history.

**Aeneas and Divine Leadership:** As Brutus is descended from Aeneas, who himself was depicted as both a warrior and a figure of destiny in Roman history, there's a direct connection between Brutus's warrior and priestly roles and the tradition of divinely sanctioned leaders from Troy.

## 5. Symbolic Role of the Priest-King or Warrior-Priest, Mediator

**Between Worlds:** As a Priest-King or Warrior-Priest, Brutus's role would have been to mediate between the divine and the mortal worlds. In ancient societies, leaders who combined spiritual and martial roles were seen as acting in accordance with the gods' will, ensuring that their rule brought balance and order to the world.

**Unity of Sacred and Secular Power:** The figure of the Priest-King symbolises the unity of sacred and secular authority, where a ruler is both the protector of the people and the spiritual guide. This is reflected in Brutus's dual role as both the lawgiver and the warrior who defends and establishes the kingdom.

# CONCLUSION

Brutus's designation as a Priest-King or Warrior-Priest reflects the ancient and historical tradition of rulers who wielded both spiritual authority and military power. His role was not merely to conquer but to found and govern a kingdom in harmony with divine will, a common theme in ancient kingship where rulers were seen as sacred figures with a mandate from the gods. In Brutus's case, his Trojan lineage, his conquest of Britain, and his establishment of laws all contribute to his identity as a figure who embodies the ideal of sacred kingship, where leadership is both a spiritual duty and a military responsibility.

## "Codes of Brutus"

The "Codes of Brutus" refer to the historical laws attributed to Brutus of Troy, a historical figure believed to have founded Britain around 1100 B.C. According to British history, Brutus being a descendant of Aeneas, a Trojan hero.

The details of the "Codes of Brutus" are largely symbolic and wrapped in historical narratives, with little historical documentation of their specific content. However, they are often referred to in later medieval British texts, especially those dealing with the founding of Britain and its early laws.

These laws were supposedly rooted in notions of justice, honour, and governance, forming the foundation of British civilisation. Some key ideas that later writers associated with the "Codes of Brutus" include:

**Establishment of Order:** Brutus is credited with establishing laws that helped create social order, guiding the moral and civic duties of the people.

**What It Represents:** The idea behind this code is the creation of a structured society. Brutus is often credited with bringing civilisation and law to the wild land of Britain. This theme suggests that he established rules for governance, organising people into a community where their rights and responsibilities were clearly defined.

**Deeper Significance:** In many ancient cultures, the arrival of a lawgiver or founder figure is symbolised by their ability to bring order to chaos. Brutus's role, therefore, is seen as that of a civilising force. The laws he established would have been concerned with basic societal organisation, such as setting up councils or assemblies and establishing a legal hierarchy. Although details are sparse, it's likely these laws aimed to foster peace and cooperation within the early communities of Britain.

**Possible Historical Echoes:** In many later legal systems, including the English common law, this theme is echoed in the idea that law brings predictability and peace to a society. This historical foundation may have inspired later ideas about governance and rule of law in Britain.

**Rights of the People:** Some traditions assert that Brutus gave laws that protected the rights of the inhabitants of Britain, offering a primitive form of governance.

**What It Represents:** Brutus is also said to have given laws that protected the rights of individuals within his new kingdom. This aspect of the code emphasises the balance between authority and individual liberty, suggesting that even in these ancient laws, there was a recognition of the people's rights.

**Deeper Significance:** The rights of the people could refer to several things: the right to own property, the right to personal safety, or even the right to fair treatment under whatever system of governance existed. Although we lack specific texts, this theme suggests that Brutus's laws were not purely authoritarian. Instead, they would have incorporated principles of fairness, setting a precedent for the later development of British liberties.

**Possible Historical Echoes:** This theme aligns with later ideas about British law, especially in medieval times when concepts like Magna Carta emerged, ensuring that even kings were subject to the law and that subjects had certain inalienable rights. It's possible that the history of Brutus and his codes were retroactively used to justify such legal evolutions.

Foundation of Monarchy: Brutus is also tied to the establishment of kingship and centralised authority in Britain, which was supposedly passed down to future rulers.

**What It Represents:** The third code, often attributed to Brutus, is the establishment of kingship and monarchy. This code focuses on the need for a centralised authority to lead and protect the people. It implies that Brutus not only laid down the law but also instituted the role of the king as a protector and lawgiver.

**Deeper Significance:** Kingship in ancient societies was often seen as divinely sanctioned, and Brutus's establishment of a monarchy could suggest that he was viewed as both a political and spiritual leader. His role as a ruler who both protected his people and embodied the law would have been central to early British history. The king, in this context, was the ultimate enforcer of the law and the source of justice.

**Possible Historical Echoes:** The establishment of monarchy by Brutus set a precedent for the idea that rulers in

Britain were responsible for upholding justice and ensuring the welfare of their sovereign people. This history may have influenced later justifications of royal authority, framing kings as central figures who derive their power from a deep and ancient tradition of lawgiving.

## Broader Implications

Though largely historical, the "Codes of Brutus" represent more than just a set of specific laws. They symbolised the foundations of British civilisation: order, rights, and governance. These ideas are reflected in the much later development of legal systems in Britain, such as the common law tradition and constitutional monarchy.

### In short:

- **Order:** Brutus established a society governed by rules.
- **Rights:** His laws protected individuals, setting early ideals of fairness.
- **Monarchy:** Brutus laid the groundwork for kingship, with rulers responsible for justice and protection.

These codes represent Britain's historical origins, providing a narrative for the later development of British legal and political traditions.

While there is no direct record of the specific contents of these codes, they served as a historical precursor to later British legal traditions, such as those attributed to Dunvallo Molmutius in the 5th century B.C., who was said to have formalised or reinforced Brutus's laws.

Dyfnwal Moelmud (also known as Dunvallo Molmutius) is credited with creating the Molmutine Laws, which became an important part of British legal tradition, particularly in Wales and among Celtic societies. These laws, though largely historical and filtered through medieval retellings, are often considered foundational and have been cited as an early precursor to Britain's later constitutional laws. Although the actual content of these laws is speculative, based on various sources such as Geoffrey of Monmouth and Welsh traditions, certain key principles attributed to Dyfnwal Moelmud's laws can be viewed as early constitutional ideas.

Key Molmutine Laws That Could Be Viewed as Constitutional

## Sanctuary (Right of Refuge)

**What It Was:** One of the most well-known aspects of the Molmutine Laws was the right of sanctuary. Certain places, such as churches, temples, and particularly roads, were designated as sanctuaries where people could seek protection, even if they had committed a crime. This meant that a person fleeing from violence or persecution could not be harmed while in these protected spaces.

**Constitutional Importance:** This early concept of sanctuary reflects later developments in British legal tradition regarding the right to safety and protection under the law, even for those accused of crimes. It laid the groundwork for ideas of legal immunity and places of refuge, which evolved in Britain's common law system.

### Freedom of Movement

**What It Was:** Dyfnwal Moelmud's laws established protected passage for travellers along certain public roads, which were considered inviolable. Anyone using these roads, even if they were an enemy or an outlaw, was supposed to be immune from harm while traveling on them.

**Constitutional Importance:** This law reflects an early form of what could later become the right to freedom of movement. In Britain's evolving legal tradition, this could be seen as a precursor to ensuring that citizens have a right to travel freely without undue interference.

### Equal Rights Under the Law

**What It Was:** Another important principle in the Molmutine Laws was the concept of fairness and equity in legal matters. The laws supposedly applied equally to all classes of people, ensuring that justice was impartial, regardless of rank or wealth.

**Constitutional Importance:** This can be seen as an early form of equal protection under the law, a key constitutional principle. Later British constitutional developments, particularly in common law, emphasised that no one, not even the monarch, is above the law—a principle reflected in Magna Carta and beyond.

## Protection of Women

**What It Was:** The Molmutine Laws reportedly provided protections for women, particularly in matters of marriage and inheritance. It is said that they ensured women had certain rights that were recognised and protected by law, such as the right to their own property.

**Constitutional Importance:** This is an early recognition of women's legal rights within a society that historically limited their autonomy. While Britain's full recognition of women's rights evolved much later, this aspect of the Molmutine Laws might represent a foundational acknowledgment of the legal status of women.

## Inheritance and Property Laws

**What It Was:** Dyfnwal Moelmud is credited with creating laws regarding the inheritance of property, which ensured the orderly transmission of wealth and land within families. These laws were meant to prevent disputes and ensure stability in family and societal structures.

**Constitutional Importance:** The regulation of inheritance and property rights became a cornerstone of British legal tradition. This early focus on property rights reflects the later importance of property law in the development of British constitutional principles, where land ownership and its protection became a fundamental right.

## Trial and Justice System

**What It Was:** According to tradition, the Molmutine Laws established basic legal processes for resolving disputes, including trials and the use of testimony to determine guilt or innocence. These processes were seen as a way to maintain justice and order within the community.

**Constitutional Importance:** The principle of fair trial and due process can be seen here, which became central to British constitutional law. The idea of using legal proceedings to determine justice in a structured manner laid the groundwork for the development of the British judicial system.

## Protection of the Vulnerable (Widows and Orphans)

**What It Was:** One of the more humanitarian aspects of the Molmutine Laws was the protection offered to widows, orphans, and the vulnerable. The laws ensured that these individuals had legal protection and could not be exploited or left without means of support.

**Constitutional Importance:** This concept is aligned with later ideas about social protection and welfare, ensuring that the state or community had a duty to protect those who were disadvantaged or at risk. British law would later incorporate this through various welfare provisions and legal protections.

## Punishment and Restitution

**What It Was:** The Molmutine Laws emphasised that punishment should be proportionate to the crime, and they also made provisions for restitution. For example, in cases of theft, the criminal might be required to repay the victim rather than face harsh physical punishment.

**Constitutional Importance:** This can be seen as a precursor to proportional justice and restorative justice, where the emphasis is not only on punishment but also on compensating the victim and maintaining social order through fairness. British law would later evolve this concept into ideas about just punishment and reparations.

## Respect for the Land

**What It Was:** Another principle attributed to Dyfnwal Moelmud was the respect for the land and the natural environment. The laws reportedly included provisions to ensure that people did not harm the land or resources recklessly, recognising the importance of environmental stewardship.

**Constitutional Importance:** This could be viewed as an early understanding of environmental law, where later British law would come to recognise the need to protect natural resources and the environment for future generations.

## Broader Constitutional Implications

While the Molmutine Laws were not a constitution in the modern sense, many of the principles attributed to Dyfnwal

Moelmud can be seen as early prototypes of constitutional norms that would develop in Britain:

**Rule of Law:** One of the fundamental ideas in these laws is that society should be governed by established rules, not by arbitrary decisions. This idea evolved into the British constitutional principle that everyone, including rulers, is subject                    to                    the                    law.

**Protection of Rights:** Whether it was the right of sanctuary, protection of the vulnerable, or ensuring equal rights under the law, the Molmutine Laws reflect an early recognition that the law should protect individuals' rights. This would eventually develop into formal legal protections such as habeas corpus and the Bill of Rights (1689).

**Justice and Fairness:** The emphasis on proportional punishment and restitution indicates that justice must be fair and equitable, concepts that became central to British common                                                              law.

## Conclusion

Dyfnwal Moelmud's laws, while historical and rooted in early Celtic traditions, contain elements that align with later constitutional principles in Britain. These include the right to protection, equal treatment under the law, property rights, and the rule of law itself. Although these laws evolved and became formalised over centuries, the Molmutine Laws reflect a foundational ethos that shaped the British legal and constitutional framework.

# THE NINE
# GENERATIONS:

There is a tradition in Britain that connects Brutus with the concept of "nine generations," where each generation is given a symbolic meaning. This idea stems from early Celtic and druidic traditions, where time, history, and ancestry were deeply intertwined with cosmology and moral values.

The "nine generations" refer to the cyclical understanding of human life and society, each representing different stages of human experience, growth, and responsibility. Although there are no direct, detailed records specifically enumerating the names and meanings of these generations in ancient texts, we can interpret them through the lens of British history and general druidic philosophy.

### Breakdown of the Nine Generations

### The First Generation: The Ancestors

**Meaning:** The first generation represents the origins and the deep connection to the past. These are the forebears, those who came before and laid the foundations for society. They symbolise wisdom, tradition, and the root of cultural identity.

**Role:** Ancestors serve as guides and protectors of the people. They provide the historical and moral context from which future generations derive meaning.

## The Second Generation: The Warriors

**Meaning:** This generation embodies strength, courage, and protection. Warriors are the defenders of their people and their laws. They take on the responsibility of safeguarding the society and its values.

**Role:** Warriors ensure the survival of the community, both physically and morally, through their valour and loyalty.

## The Third Generation: The Farmers/Providers

**Meaning:** Farmers symbolise fertility, sustenance, and the nurturing of the land. This generation is tasked with providing for the community, ensuring that the people are well-fed and that the resources of the earth are respected and replenished.

**Role:** Providers cultivate the land, securing the means of life and symbolising the close bond between humans and nature.

## The Fourth Generation: The Artisans/Craftsmen

**Meaning:** Artisans represent creativity, skill, and the ability to transform raw materials into tools, art, and functional objects. This generation is associated with innovation and culture.

**Role:** The craftsmen not only produce goods necessary for life but also elevate society through art and technology, fostering development and the refinement of culture.

## The Fifth Generation: The Scholars/Teachers

**Meaning:** This generation embodies knowledge, education, and the transmission of wisdom. They are the keepers of knowledge and tradition, ensuring that important cultural and intellectual values are passed down to future generations.

**Role:** Teachers and scholars are responsible for the moral and intellectual growth of society, ensuring the continuity of wisdom through learning.

## The Sixth Generation: The Rulers/Lawgivers

**Meaning:** The rulers or lawgivers are those who embody justice, leadership, and the organisation of society. This generation represents authority, responsibility, and the creation of laws that bind and protect the people.

**Role:** Lawgivers like Molmutius himself create the legal and social structures that allow for a stable and harmonious community.

## The Seventh Generation: The Priests/Druids

**Meaning:** The seventh generation is spiritual in nature, representing the druids or priests who serve as the intermediaries between the divine and the earthly realms. They are connected to the gods, the forces of nature, and the deeper cosmic truths.

**Role:** Priests maintain the spiritual health of society, offering guidance, performing rituals, and maintaining the connection to the spiritual world.

## The Eighth Generation: The Traders/Merchants

**Meaning:** This generation represents commerce, trade, and the exchange of goods and ideas. Traders connect different parts of society and different cultures, facilitating communication, prosperity, and the sharing of knowledge.

**Role:** Merchants expand the horizons of the community, not only through trade but also through the exchange of ideas, fostering relationships between different peoples.

## The Ninth Generation: The Children/Youth

**Meaning:** The final generation represents renewal, potential, and the future. The children are those who will carry forward the legacy of all previous generations, embodying hope and the promise of continued growth and progress.

**Role:** The youth are responsible for inheriting the wisdom and accomplishments of their ancestors and will eventually take on the roles of the previous generations, continuing the cycle.

# SYMBOLIC IMPORTANCE OF THE NINE GENERATIONS

The nine generations form a complete cycle, where each generation plays a vital role in the overall stability, continuity, and prosperity of society. In many ancient traditions, the number nine is sacred and represents completeness or wholeness. In this context, each generation complements the others, ensuring that society remains balanced and sustainable.

This concept can also be seen as a reflection of the different stages of human life, from birth to death, and the roles we assume in the course of our existence. From youth to elder, each stage brings different responsibilities and values, mirroring the way these nine generations contribute to the survival and evolution of the community.

To truly claim an indigenous identity within British society, it is essential for individuals to delve deeply into their ancestral roots, tracing their lineage as far back as nine generations. This journey through one's family history not only serves to reinforce a sense of belonging but also strengthens the connection to heritage, culture, and the ancient ties that bind them to the land. By exploring nine generations, individuals can uncover the rich tapestry of their lineage, situating themselves within a broader historical context that donors the legacy of those who came before them. This depth of understanding contributes to a more profound recognition of identity, rooted in the shared history, customs, and values passed down through generations.

The "Codes of Brutus" (1100 B.C.) and the laws of Dyfnwal Moelmud (450 B.C.) should indeed be viewed through the lens of early legal history, with their significance being largely symbolic rather than strictly legal. These ancient codes represent foundational ideals, reflecting early concepts of justice, governance, and social order that once held great influence over British society.

As we confront the modern challenges of corruption, disillusionment with Parliament, and widespread legal issues that leave many feeling unheard, it may be time to revisit the principles our ancestors established. By looking back at these early laws and customs, we have the opportunity to rediscover a set of moral and ethical foundations that once united the people of this land. In these turbulent times, reconnecting with the values embedded in the "Codes of Brutus" and the laws of Dyfnwal Moelmud could inspire a revival of the original integrity, ethics, and customs that characterised ancient Britain. Revamping these timeless principles, even as a guiding framework, could provide a path toward restoring the sense of justice, community, and resilience that has long been part of the British heritage.